Apartment in Paris

To Nancy with
fond regards
Ros 4/98

Apartment in Paris

By Erasmus H. Kloman

RENTING,

ROAMING,

WINING,

AND DINING,

• UNITED PUBLISHERS GROUP, NORWALK, CONNECTICUT •
• JUDD PUBLISHING, WASHINGTON, D.C. •

Cover design by Anne Masters Design, Inc.
Text design by Pauline Neuwirth, Neuwirth & Associates

Published by Judd Publishing, Inc.
United Publishers Group
50 Washington Street
Norwalk, CT 06854

Printed and bound in United States of America

Library of Congress Cataloging-in-Publication Data is available
ISBN: 0-8038-9420-1

Table of Contents

Foreword

𝒯his is a brilliant picture of Paris, bound to delight its readers whether they know and love France or are considering a first trip. Beyond an American audience, the book will appeal to English-speaking travelers from around the globe.

The author, an artist, and his wife, an inspired cook, have rented a small apartment every year for nine years sight unseen. Sometimes they find themselves located in the shadow of Notre-Dame, with the Seine flowing below them and the history of medieval Paris in the air they breathe. Another year they are in the heart of commercial Paris in a neighborhood mainly serving the garment trade. In every case the author explores the French character as easily and wittily as he does the city, and offers excellent advice. He considers that taking the Metro gives the visitor "great psychic rewards," and suggests that a pair of ear plugs are essential equipment for the tourist who is attempting to find sleep in a Left Bank hotel or apartment of a merry weekend night.

This is a guidebook in that the reader learns how to rent an apartment, how to explore restaurants ranging from the grand to the humble, and how to market for picnics or meals in the apartment with the help of Suzanne Kloman's recipes and culinary tips. There are vivid descriptions of historic sites not only in Paris but within easy range of the city. Not to be missed is the chapter on the adventures of renting a car for a sightseeing expedition.

The chapter on finding the right apartment for your budget and the appendices at the end of the book are especially useful for anyone interested in following the Klomans' footsteps. Here readers will find a primer on apartment renting and a methodical supplement to the many topics covered in the text.

Mr. Kloman's light touch never deserts him, and while his practical advice is wonderfully sound, this charming book is a romantic story.

Susan Mary Alsop
February, 1998
Washington, D.C.

Acknowledgments

Many collaborators helped in bringing this book into print. First of all I must acknowledge my ever willing and resourceful traveling companion, the keeper of the diaries on which much of the text is based, the gourmet cook who furnished the recipes embedded in the text, my in-house art critic, the skilled editor of more drafts than I care to number, the one who encourages my creative pursuits while steering me away from some of my zanier ideas, my dear wife Suzanne. The book is really our joint offspring.

Three people who assisted on my last book, *Sojourn in Gascony*, were involved in producing this book. Lynne Shaner edited an early draft for style. Ruina Judd served with her remarkable flair in all aspects of the publishing process, and once again I am deeply endebted to Patricia Hass for her counsel on the ways of the publishing world.

Thanks are due to the staff of the library of the French Embassy, especially Gary M. Dwor-Frécaut, Antoine Bussy and Felix Ferrant and to the French Government Tourist Office in New York, especially André Moraillon, for assistance in compiling the directory of rental agencies.

Two friends of ours shared photographs of Paris which inspired twelve of my paintings. Professional photographer, Leslie Clevenger, and her husband, the Honorable Raymond Charles Clevenger III, Judge of the U.S. Court of Appeals for the Federal Circuit, and also an ace photographer, take frequent biking trips to France. With an infallible eye for the whimsical and off-beat as well as for the quintessentially Parisian, they have assembled a vast photographic archive from which I chose twelve subjects for my paintings. I am deeply indebted to them not only for what their cameras captured but also for the good times enjoyed in our collaboration.

Two instructors at the Art League in Alexandria, Virginia, Diane Tessler and Rick Weaver, guided me throughout much of the period when this book was in the making. Of the many great teachers I have had, they stand out for their enthusiasm and unusual ability to enter with you into the world of the painting.

In the process of writing I had to meet the daunting challenge of shifting from my old computer to a new one. Monica Hammock, who served as my guru during this period, came to my rescue on many occasions and actually made what could have been an angst-ridden transition into a fulfilling experience.

Many friends and associates have read all or parts of the manuscript in its various iterations, and their comments have been reflected in the process of revision. Special thanks are due to Daniel Blondy, John Cuadrado, Nicholas and Judy Doman, Philip Geyelin, Rochelle Jaffe, Ward Kirchwein, Alexander Kloman and Danielle Dyer Kloman, Sylvie Boutet de Monvel, Polly Platt, Felicia Rogan, Laura Delano Roosevelt, Jean-Pierre Szabo, and Denie Weil.

While gratefully acknowledging their thoughtful contributions, I recognize that responsibility for the final text remains solely with me.

Erasmus H. Kloman

Preface

$\mathcal{T}$hose who cherish Paris come from all corners of the globe, and they visit their beloved city in the greatest numbers during the summer months. But Paris can be beguiling year round, and many foreigners make it a point to visit when fewer tourists are about.

Suzanne, my wife, and I have been able to spend some time in Paris during each of the past fourteen years, usually in the autumn, though we agree with songwriter Cole Porter who loved Paris "every moment of the year."

More people visit Paris than any other destination on earth, and the number of American tourists has grown to two and a half million a year. The rest of France is, of course, a powerful magnet for worldwide tourism, and most who travel there spend at least a little time in Paris.

In our earlier Parisian sojourns we stayed at hotels, mainly on the left bank, and, since we always travel on a limited budget, we gravitated to the smaller and more reasonably priced establishments. Our favorite became the charming Duc de St. Simon in the seventh *arrondissement*, (one of the twenty districts into which Paris was divided in 1870). This hotel is so highly prized by a faithful clientele that to obtain our first reservation we had to overcome what seemed an insurmountable "Catch

22", an apparent hotel policy that welcomed only people who had stayed there previously. In 1986, a year when tourism dropped off sharply due to fear of terrorism, we managed to get a reservation, and we returned happily for several years to the St. Simon until their prices began to creep up and we ventured into the practice of renting apartments.

Hotel rates in Paris (averaging $265 a night according to a 1997 survey) are among the highest in the world exceeded only by such cities as Tokyo and Hong Kong. In 1989, hoping to save a few francs (we calculate that our per night lodging usually comes to around half that of a mid-range hotel) while also becoming more a part of *la vie Parisienne*, we signed up for the first of our annual week-long apartment rentals located mainly in central Paris.

Our first landlords were American friends who rent out their apartment at reasonable rates whenever they are not in residence. With each rental experience we gain new knowledge and expertise helping us cope with the occasional perplexities facing foreigners. We now know our way around our favorite parts of the city well enough to feel at home, and we find the Parisians we encounter far more gracious. (Is it we or they who have changed the most?) Looking back now, memories of the good times have dimmed the memory of some pretty awful moments when we confronted unfamiliar transportation systems, citywide transportation strikes, terrorist bombs, out-of-order telephones, or contrary household appliances. We are proud to have met each of these challenges without pushing the panic button. The more we learn about the practical business of living as renters the more we relax and enjoy what Paris has to offer.

Each successive visit also finds us better able to select where to go, people and sights to see, and how to spend each day. In general we like to do the kinds of things most Parisians enjoy—dining well in favorite restaurants (mostly avoiding the very pricey and pretentious places), strolling and window-shopping along the avenues and back streets, visiting museums and galleries, or taking a day trip to one of the many scenic and historic sites on the outskirts of the city. Whenever we get the chance, we love nothing better than to engage in a favorite Parisian pastime, people-watching from a sidewalk café. Last, but by no means least, is the adventure of searching out the best *patisseries, épiceries, charcuteries, marchands de vins, or fromagers* in our neighborhood and savoring unhurried meals *chez nous*. Simple joys all, and we treasure them.

Weather in autumn when we are in Paris is not very different from Washington or New York. Although we have encountered plenty of cloudy or rainy spells, we are usually blessed with at least several days of glorious sunshine. A sunny day in Paris with the scents of autumn in the air is pure bliss. Perhaps because Paris is still very much a walking city and every Parisian is at heart a *flâneur* (a stroller or lounger in a favorite café), weather is a matter of consuming interest to everyone. The trim figures of most Parisians undoubtedly owe much to their fondness for walking.

To further understand our love affair with Paris you need look no further than the ineffable beauty of its cityscape. In addition to its magnificent location straddling the glorious Seine there is its stunning architecture; and we are both enthusiastic architecture buffs even if not professionally trained. Buildings in classical design extend along avenues as far as the eye can see in sweeping perspectives especially in the areas laid out by Baron Haussmann, the master planner under Napoleon III. But we also love walking in the areas where the architects were at liberty to do their own thing, even though quite a few modernized store fronts and other superficial facelifts have lost whatever appeal they may have had when they were performed.

Even such everyday activities as mastering the Metro and other means of transportation can bring great psychic returns. The Parisian *Métropolitain* is considered one of the world's most user-friendly systems with signage and route maps designed to steer passengers confidently through the labyrinthian passages. The 15 Metro lines with their 124 miles of track serve 370 stations so that no point in the capital is more than 550 yards from a Metro station. We also rely on certain bus routes and enjoy riding above ground to observe the ever-intriguing sights of the city. The RER, *(Réseau Express Régional)*, an express 'metro' network, consists of four lines serving points within the city as well as more distant destinations, including the airports. It is convenient for excursions to places described in the pages that follow such as Saint-Germain-en-Laye, Versailles, or Chatou. We rely on taxis only in the late evening, for getting to and from the airport or when it's raining, if we can find one.

Each year we feel a little more integrated into Parisian life. We have gradually expanded our circle of acquaintances, a mix of American and British expatriates (the diverse American community numbers between twenty and thirty thousand, while the British count is even higher) and a few native Parisians, including our closest friend Sylvie, whom Suzanne has known for many years. Having learned something about how to rent apartments and to live well on a limited budget, we thought our experience might be helpful to others. This book can be read as a primer on apartment living and economical ways to enjoy daily life in Paris. It includes comments on our favorite restaurants, tips on cooking in apartment kitchens, recipes favored by Suzanne, and advice on shopping in the many specialty stores and the supermarkets.

The discussions of cuisine and the sixteen recipes scattered throughout the text give due recognition to the singular importance of cuisine and the art of the table in all of France and especially in Paris. Suzanne is an accomplished and knowledgeable cook with a special facility for French cuisine. Our years of travel to the wellspring of this cuisine have enhanced our appreciation of it. We continue to be fascinated by the *paradoxe français*—the extraordinary fact that despite their rich diet and high consumption of alcoholic beverages French men and women generally retain good health and trim figures. The rate of heart disease in France is reported to be three times lower than in the United States.

Scientific efforts to identify the cause of this phenomenon have generally focused on the French preference for red as opposed to white wine. Other factors deserving consideration are the great amount of walking and other exercise in the average Frenchman's daily life, and the attention the French pay to personal style. The latest studies show, moreover, that people in the southern regions, where the preference for red over white wine and olive oil over butter for cooking is much greater than in the north, live healthier and longer lives.

In recent decades both sides of the Atlantic have undergone something of a revolution in cooking and eating habits with growing awareness of the importance of diet to health and well-being. Today most French chefs have veered away from classic *haute cuisine* with its cream, butter, sugar and pastry while inventing delicious and less fattening treatments of dishes, though quite a few traditionalists still hold to the old ways. Not many Parisian restaurant menus offer what we call a "low-cal" choice, but experienced diners can detect which dishes are richer than others. Suzanne eschews low-cal cooking though she is a firm believer in a healthy and balanced diet. While some of her recipes in the following pages specify cream, butter and sugar, she proposes other dishes without these rich ingredients.

A concluding chapter helps you find the right apartment for your budget among the many publications and other resources available. This book should make it easier for you to find an apartment meeting your needs and to enjoy your new abode once you're settled in.

The almost infinite variety of rental apartments means that something suitable can be found for all types of renters. Though Suzanne and I have selected places meeting our needs and life style as a married couple, apartment rentals can work well for singles, pairs, families with children, or even groups. We hope this book will meet the needs of a diverse readership wanting to enjoy the many rewards we have found during our Parisian sojourns.

The appendices include a directory of agencies offering apartment rentals, a checklist of phone numbers and information to help renters with daily activity or possible emergencies, notes on suggested reading, Internet web sites providing a wealth of data on Paris and France, a list of restaurants, and lists of places of interest cited in the text. More English-speaking tourists and other foreigners are renting apartments in Paris than ever before. Many thousands of units of all kinds in a wide price range and in nearly all parts of the city become temporary homes for people like Suzanne and me. For the limited effort that goes into selecting, lining up and maintaining an apartment the rewards are tremendous. Many of our rentals over the past nine years have been for just one week, a minimum required by many, but not all, rental agencies. As a week draws to a close we invariably find that it has not been long enough. We look forward to a time when we can stay a good deal longer.

Although our apartments have been situated in only four of the twenty arrondissements, we have seen enough of the city to know the areas that suit our tastes and pocketbook. We have also learned to cope as most Parisians do with challenges such as terrorist bombs, the worst of which were the Algerian-made devices exploded in Paris in 1995 close to the apartment we had just vacated. But on average the rate of homicides in Paris is far lower than in most American cities and only about one-fifth that of our own home town, Washington, DC. The ratio of police to population in Paris far exceeds that of most American or English cities.

In some ways public order in Paris suffers more disruption from strikes organized by labor unions and protest manifestations by a seemingly endless array of disaffected citizens. An estimated one hundred thousand people participated in the December 1995 strikes that brought normal patterns of life to an abrupt halt. A kindly disposed observer has asked: "Would it be the France we love without a few *grèves* (strikes) here and there?" Parisians seem to have mastered the art of coping by pretending that nothing unusual is happening and, at the same time, maintaining their right to rail against perceived offenders of the social order. We observe from the sidelines while relishing the fun and excitement of making a Paris apartment our temporary abode. This book will make it possible for you to do the same.

Erasmus H. Kloman

Ile de la Cité

Our first apartment on the Ile de la Cité came highly recommended by friends who had previously rented it. We were confident that its American owners, also friends of ours, would have equipped it with everything we might need without sacrificing the French flair in the ambiance. Indeed, we enjoyed our week in this apartment so much that after our first stay we took it a second time.

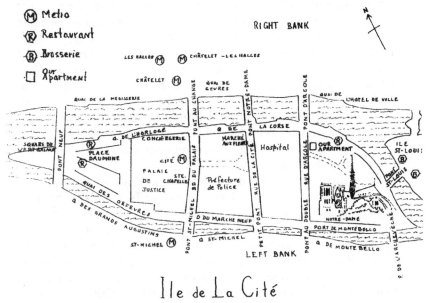

Ile de La Cité

The Ile de la Cité apartment is close to the sixth and seventh *arrondissements*, our favorite part of the city. Over the years we had stayed in this area in various small hotels, and our friend Sylvie's house is in the seventh. Actually, the Ile de la Cité is divided between the fourth and the first arrondissements but only a short walk to our old haunts. During earlier visits we had strolled around the island, touring such landmarks as Notre-Dame and Sainte-Chapelle, and lunching in restaurants on the Place Dauphine, a tranquil little nook near the western end of the island.

A VIEW WORTH THE CLIMB

We moved into our first apartment well after midnight and our arrival in the dark was something of a nightmare. We had flown to Paris from Munich and, on the advice of friends, took the RER from the airport to the stop, St-Michel/Notre-Dame closest to our apartment. Adding to the heft of our bags were several weighty Viennese Sacher tortes (each packed in a heavy wooden box) brought as presents for Parisian friends. Totally baffled by the mazelike layout of the St-Michel station, we made several abortive attempts to reach the street but ran into exits that were temporarily closed, escalators going the wrong way, and a non-working elevator. As frustration mounted and our huffing and puffing grew more audible, two young men ran toward us at the foot of a long stairway we were wearily preparing to climb. They seized our bags and dashed up to the top of the stairs out of our sight. For a terrible moment we wondered if we had seen the last of our bags. But up on the street we found these two good lads neatly stacking our luggage and waiting to wish us well. We thanked them profusely before they hurried off into the darkness. Since this act of good will we have been blessed by countless acts of courtesy and kindness on the part of Parisians, while our encounters with rude behavior have been quite rare.

Alone in the darkness we wondered exactly where we were, and where was #9 rue d'Arcole and our apartment? In a moment the enormous silhouette of Notre-Dame against the night sky gave us a bearing. While Suzanne waited anxiously on the sidewalk with our pile of luggage I scouted around and found the route to the apartment. Having located the building, we still had to drag the bags across the Place du Parvis in front of the cathedral and down the street to our doorway. The final ordeal was the struggle up four flights of a narrow circular stairway lit dimly for three minute intervals controlled by a central timer. Between intervals we were plunged into pitch darkness as we scrambled to find the light switches. (These devilish devices called *minuteries* are common also in corridors and other public spaces or apartment houses and smaller hotels throughout Paris. Energy-conscious Parisians patiently accept this method of saving electricity probably without seeing the irony of their existence in the City of Light.) Only after our rental of this apartment did we learn that our friends who own it get in shape for the four flights by an annual mountain climbing vacation in Switzerland.

Once inside the apartment, though frazzled, we exulted in having arrived but were too tired to make more than a quick survey before bed. The next morning brought the thrill of waking up above the rooftops in the very heart of Paris. Our windows afforded views in nearly every direction. We reveled in all the typically Parisian sensual messages—dramatic sights of the Seine and its bridges, green parks and tree-lined streets, countless church spires; the sounds of Paris traffic and the busy shop-keepers competing for attention with the clamorous ringing of the Cathedral chimes; and the marvelous aromas wafting our way from the street where the scent of autumn leaves mingled with that of croissants and other bakery delicacies.

Like children playing house, we checked out the apartment—bedroom, bath, living room, dining room, and kitchen—compact but very comfortable, simply but charmingly furnished. There were shelves full of guidebooks, other books and articles on Paris, and guest books with notes and helpful advice from previous renters. This was indeed what we had dreamed of, and the ordeal of the night before was almost forgotten.

We made a shopping list and hurried down for our first Parisian breakfast. Crossing the Place du Parvis in front of the Cathedral we walked over a bridge to the left bank and settled on one of numerous cafés. Croissants, a baguette, marmalade, coffee, and orange juice never tasted better. Thus energized, we located a collection of shops on Place Maubert for all our grocery needs. Later we found that this is the site of a thrice-weekly open-air market. (We did our marketing here during our first stay on La Cité, as the island is called today, until we discovered how much easier it was to go to the close-by Ile St-Louis.) With shopping bags full we again climbed the four flights to our apartment, thankful not to be carrying the same load as the night before.

The rue d'Arcole runs past the front of the Cathedral across the

Pont d'Arcole to the right bank. Along the street a tawdry collection of sidewalk vendors and shops noisily hawk souvenirs of Notre-Dame and other famous landmarks. It was always a welcome relief to escape into our building and upstairs to the serene atmosphere of our apartment. Steps away from the streets lined with souvenir vendors the less traveled back streets offer a tranquil retreat.

This area, called the Ancien Cloître, is the only surviving reminder of how the residential areas of La Cité looked during the eleventh and twelfth centuries. A cathedral school was located here, and students lived in the houses of the canons. The almost palpable sense of the past provides sharp and welcome contrast to the hubub of the nearby street vendors and tourists.

Deep Roots in the Past

La Cité has been continually inhabited since prehistoric times, and the Gallic tribe of the Parisii settled there in the third century BC. Then called Lutetia, meaning "habitation between the waters," it was connected to both banks by two wooden bridges. Under the Pax Romana the town spread to the left bank, while the marshland (Marais) on the right bank remained largely uninhabited. Barbarian invasions in the second century AD left Lutetia in ruins, but it was rebuilt toward the end of that century.

In the fifth century the Franks became the masters of Paris, and rather than destroying what the Romans had built they adapted to the more advanced Roman civilization. Under Clovis, the sixth-century ruler who settled in La Cité, the Franks converted to Christianity and became even more closely tied to Rome.

During the Middle Ages, from approximately the ninth to the fourteenth century, Paris was an agricultural center, and the Cité was the principal market for produce from the surrounding countryside. The Marais was drained for raising vegetables and grains. Fish were brought in from the north and game from the forests. Medieval Paris also witnessed the building of Notre-Dame (1163–1345) and other churches on the island and nearby banks. These ancient landmarks exert a strong pull into the past on a visitor today, and countless hours can be spent exploring the wonders of their confines.

Ile de la Cité is just a little more than one kilometer long and composed of three distinct areas, each with its own character. As shown on the map, the western end comprises the open spaces of the Square du

Vert Galant (Henri IV) and the Place Dauphine as well as the monumental complexes housing the Palais de Justice, Sainte-Chapelle and the Conciergerie. The middle of the island contains administrative buildings such as the Préfecture de Police, the Tribunal de Commerce, and the hospital, all designed under the guidance of renowned architect and city-planner Baron Haussmann in the nineteenth century during the reigns of Louis-Philippe and Napoleon III. To make way for these ambitious construction projects as well as the square facing the cathedral, some twenty-five thousand people were evacuated from their ancient and mostly decaying houses. The great cathedral of Notre-Dame and its adjoining park dominate the lower end of the island. Road signs marking the distance to Paris from all over France are measured from this revered landmark.

THE PALAIS DE JUSTICE

Since the Revolution, which overturned the judicial system of the Ancien Regime, the Palais de Justice has housed the national Law Courts. The present building is a nineteenth-to-twentieth century restoration of palaces serving as principal residences of the early rulers of Paris. The Roman governors, Merovingian and Capetian kings, and subsequent monarchs lived here until Charles V moved to Right Bank palaces at the Louvre and the Marais in 1358. Until the building of the Louvre as a fortress defense against the English, who controlled territory immediately to the north, La Cité was regarded as the most secure site for the royal residence. Visitors touring the Palais de Justice today can observe not only some of the courts presiding over the judicial system but also the sites where early rulers lived for one thousand years. Thus, for example, what is now the First Civil Court was once the Upper Chamber where Louis IX (Saint Louis and patron saint of France) lived and dispensed justice in the thirteenth century. The Palais de Justice complex surrounds the magnificent Sainte-Chapelle built at his command.

SAINTE-CHAPELLE

This superb example of the Gothic age graces a small courtyard within the Palais de Justice. Its towering arches, vaulted ceilings, and dazzling stained-glass windows are among the greatest joys of a visit to La Cité. Built in the amazingly short span of thirty-three months and consecrated in 1248, this chapel was designed to shelter holy relics of Christ and the Virgin. Saint Louis acquired these relics, including the alleged crown of thorns, from Baudoin, a French nobleman and the Emperor of Constantinople, in 1239. Saint Louis is said to have paid a sum over twice the cost of building the chapel to bring the relics to Paris. Those relics not destroyed during the Revolution now reside in Notre-Dame. The spire of Sainte Chappelle dates from 1853 when a successful restoration of the church was undertaken to repair the severe damage it suffered during the revolution.

The delicacy and seeming fragility of Sainte-Chapelle are remarkable in view of the fact that the basic structure has survived intact over seven centuries, yielding neither to the ravages of time nor the urban environment. Access to this landmark is more strictly controlled than at Notre-Dame, and crowds are likely to be smaller. However there can be lengthy ticket lines for the frequent musical concerts ranging from ancient liturgical to contemporary selections. Sainte-Chapelle, the towers of the Conciergerie, and its north facade are all that remain of the medieval royal palace, and the chapel has been subjected to far more sympathetic restoration and alteration than other parts of the complex. It is open daily except for Mondays.

The Conciergerie

Crossing the western end of the island is Pont Neuf, the oldest bridge across the Seine dating to 1578 and belying its name for all the intervening years. Just to the east of the bridge is the statue of Henri IV, perhaps the most beloved of all French monarchs and a particular favorite of ours.

We had first come upon his trail on a visit to his birthplace in Pau overlooking the Pyrenees. This lover of the good life and of untold numbers of his female subjects of all ranks and estates endeared himself to his people by declaring that there should be a chicken in every pot on Sunday.

Not far from the Pont Neuf and facing the Seine on the north side of the island is the Conciergerie, the high Gothic complex built, enlarged, and restored by a succession of French monarchs beginning in the thirteenth century. It was originally intended as the residence of the concierge or keeper of the king's mansion. Over successive reigns the concierge gained numerous privileges, including the right to license shops and trading stalls within the palace walls. The three round towers facing the river are all that remain of the original palace fortifications.

Inside on the ground floor, one of the most important architectural features is the huge vaulted hall of the Gentlemen-at-Arms, a unique survivor of the Gothic style applied to such a large space. This is one of three large halls built in the fourteenth century by Philip the Fair. John the Good built the kitchens and the Clock Tower around 1350. The Conciergerie served as barracks for up to six hundred soldiers. The four enormous ovens (for bread, meat, fish and vegetables) which fed these soldiers are still in place. Over the course of seven centuries the Conciergerie served as prison for thousands of condemned individuals of all ranks and classes until its conversion to an historic monument in 1914. Among its most famous victims were those incarcerated during the revolution, including Marie-Antoinette, Josephine (later Empress of France,) and Robespierre, confined there on the morning of his execution. For a while it was the site of the dreaded guillotine or the "nation's razor," so-called at the time. The guillotine blade, now hanging on the prison wall, is a grim reminder of the terror of that era. Inscribed on the walls of one room are the names of over twenty-six hundred prisoners who went from the Conciergerie to their execution.

This complex now serves as a museum; wax figures of prisoners depict daily life. A series of cells depicts the *pailleux*, the ordinary prisoners who had to sleep on piles of straw. Other cells display the few amenities that were allowed those who could pay for better accommodations. Perhaps most riveting is the reconstitution of the cell and adjoining chapel created for Marie-Antoinette where, after being separated from the King, she spent her last seventy-six days. The seated figure of the queen wearing a white morning robe holds her prayer book under the watchful eye of a uniformed guard standing behind her. Her robe is a copy of one of the two dresses left to her. It was said that when she was not praying or reading she spent her time motionless twisting her wedding ring around her finger and watching her guards in their games of cards. Today large crowds, fascinated by the gruesome reminders of the Revolution and the Reign of Terror, make the Conciergerie one of the major tourist sites on La Cité, rivaled only

by Notre-Dame. The best vantage point for viewing the whole complex is the Quai de la Méggisserie on the north bank of the Seine.

NOTRE-DAME

Built over a period of nearly two centuries, Notre-Dame was the center of medieval life—both secular and religious—in Paris. Actors presented plays on stages in the great central nave; the homeless slept in its corridors; kings and feudal lords set off for the Crusades from its brilliant portals; and great official occasions drew as many as ten thousand people. The commanding view of the surrounding terrain from the top of Notre-Dame is well worth the sometimes lengthy wait in lines and the climb up the narrow spiraling stairway. Magnificent acoustics and architectural splendor combine to draw large numbers to the vespers services and to free concerts on Sunday evenings throughout the year.

Situated near the upstream end of the island and surrounded by park and gardens, the cathedral commands attention from all angles. The large square in front of the cathedral, the Place du Parvis, provides the best-known view of the facade. Here, in addition to the imposing statue of Charlemagne is an archaeological crypt containing monuments and other vestiges dating as far back as the Gallo-Roman era, (third century BC to 360 AD) along with remnants of houses and streets of the medieval Cité.

In a little park at the tip of the island is the monument honoring all the French citizens deported abroad to grim fates of prison and/or death.

In another happier setting S. and I enjoyed a picnic overlooking the Seine and the cathedral at the end of the Pont de l'Archeveché, the westernmost bridge from the island to the left bank. Finding sites for picnics away from the crowds usually calls for a trek to one of the small parks at the western end of La Cité (the Square du Vert Galant, Henri IV) or the eastern end of the neighboring Ile St-Louis, (Square Barye) or the walkways along the river below the quais on either bank. It's an easy matter as well as good fun to pick up a bottle of wine, a baguette, some cheese, *saucisson* (sausage made perhaps by the purveyor's brother-in-law), olives, fruit, and possibly a pastry too.

THE LEFT-BANK VS RIGHT-BANK QUANDARY

Nine bridges, each with its own rich history, connect La Cité to either side of the river and to its smaller neighbor, the Ile St-Louis. From these two island locations there is always a tantalizing choice of directions to take in exploring Paris. With their dramatic setting in the middle of the Seine and their vistas up and down the river, the islands abound in visual delights for pedestrians, photographers, or artists. Among the most notable of the many Impressionists who recorded these scenes in their paintings were Caillebotte, Degas, Manet, Monet, Pissarro, Renoir and Signac.

Just walking along the wide streets on either side of the islands gives an endlessly fascinating view of the river plied by commercial boats of all sizes and shapes and by the many tourist sight-seeing boats such as the Bateaux-Mouches. The familiarity of these scenes as captured on a zillion postcards cannot detract from the wonder of actually seeing them, no matter how often.

The difference in character between the right and left banks of the Seine can be traced far back in history to the different kinds of activity concentrated in each area. The right bank developed as the mercantile quarter and still retains its business focus and its reputation for luxury. This side of the river came to be known as "The Town" whereas the left bank was called "The University" mainly because it was the site of many teaching institutions. Pope Innocent III founded the University of Paris in 1215, the first university in France, while the

Sorbonne was founded by Robert Sorbon in 1257 as a refuge for poor theology students. The Left Bank eventually became the home of intellectuals, Bohemians, and the antiestablishment, but until the end of the monarchy it was favored as a site for grand private houses or *hôtels particuliers* of the aristocracy. Many of the fashionable literary salons were held in these elegant town houses. As the locale of the Assemblée Nationale and most federal ministries the Left Bank is a center of government. The Right Bank is noted for the Louvre (fortress turned palace turned museum), the Palais Royal, the Elysée Palace (home of French presidents), the Hôtel de Ville, (city hall) and of such monumental spaces as the Place de la Concorde and Tuileries Gardens.

The distinction between the two sides, though less pronounced than in the past, is still very real, and residents are fiercely loyal to their own bank. On average, left bank buildings predate those on the right bank by about two centuries, and the aged wood in beams and crooked walls of these ancient structures appeal to many Parisians who dote on relics of the past.

The sixth and seventh arrondissements are known as the venue of "old money" whereas the fashionable more modern sixteenth arrondissement across the river is favored by those possessing newer wealth. The ultra chic suburb, Neuilly, lies just to the northwest of the sixteenth, while the Bois de Boulogne and the lesser known and under appreciated Passy-Auteuil neighborhood are within its borders. As noted above, our friend Sylvie lives on the left bank in a wonderful house, which has passed through four generations of her family. She would never consider living elsewhere, and through her we learned to love the seventh arrondissement. We generally prefer the somewhat subdued atmosphere of the left bank, largely devoid of the right bank's commercialism, which ranges from the upscale, glamorous, and glitzy to the seedy. For the last two years, however, we have rented in the Marais on the right bank.

As for American, British and other expatriates, they are scattered about in the parts of Paris according to their personal preferences, economic means and professional interests. For example, artists tend to locate around Montmartre or in Left Bank art-centered *quartiers*. Ex-foreign service people who have adopted Paris as their home base may be found both in the Left Bank areas of the sixth and seventh arrondissements and in the sixteenth. Well-heeled business people and professionals are also likely to be found in the sixteenth and in the fashionable suburb of Neuilly. Most students live on the Left Bank near the Sorbonne and the other academic institutions of this area.

PLACE DAUPHINE

Our favorite spot for quiet relaxation on La Cité is the Place Dauphine. Near the western end of the island, it is a refuge from the tourist crowds who gather mainly around the cathedral. In this triangular park surrounded by tall plane trees you may sometimes find a game of *boules* or *pétanque* (a bowling game) under way. Once a pastime enjoyed by elderly provincials, this game has now become the latest craze of younger generations. Here also are the friendly bistro Chez Paul and Caveau du Palais (one Michelin fork). Chez Paul was a favorite hang-out of Yves Montand and its atmosphere evokes the era of the great music-hall singer. However *La Belle France* in its May 1997 issue (see Appendix C) gave the food a lukewarm review. Suzanne and I were delighted to discover that our hero, Henri IV, was responsible for the creation of this hideaway at the same time he was masterminding the much larger Place Royale (now the Place des Vosges). The Place Dauphine area had been a royal orchard and occasional execution ground. In 1607 Henri ceded the land specifically to enclose a little park with a group of identical houses to be built of brick, white stone, and slate. The park was named Dauphine after the future Louis XIII. Only No. 14 still retains its original aspect. The eastern end of the enclosure was razed in 1874 to make way for a grand stairway leading up to the west front of the Palais de Justice.

The Place Dauphine and the Quai aux Fleurs on the eastern end of the island are the principal places where private apartments are occasionally available for rentals on La Cité, whereas the mainly residential Ile St-Louis has many more.

WALKING EXCURSIONS

One of our first walking expeditions led to discovery of the enchanting Ile St-Louis. Leaving the eastern tip of La Cité, just a few steps over the Pont St-Louis, we entered another world that we would later grow to love for its distinctive character and many charms. In contrast to the famous tourist attractions of La Cité, Ile St-Louis offers the charm of elegant residential neighborhoods and off-beat boutiques. During the week it is usually free of crowds, and those that come are more likely to be Parisians than foreign tourists. On weekends and holidays the Pont St-Louis connecting the two islands is the setting for mime shows, in-line skate races, and artists painting in the hope of a few sales to curious passersby.

A single interior street, rue St-Louis-en-l'Ile, bisects the island lengthwise east to west. On this and some of the cross streets is a variety of food and wine shops and other establishments offering in their wares an escape from the ordinary. Weird and wonderful toys for young and old, one-of-a-kind "wearable art" clothing and jewelry, and numerous galleries offering a range from traditional to off-the-wall artworks, all make for fascinating strolling and shopping. We have noticed over the years, however, a fairly high rate of turnover among some of these shops. For example, what once was the Salon de Thé in

the sketch below is now a bookstore dedicated exclusively to poetry.

We did most of our shopping on Ile St-Louis during our second stay on La Cité and liked this smaller more intimate island so much that we selected it for two future rental apartments.

If apartment renters should wish guided walking tours they can contact the Office of Tourism at the number noted in the checklist at Appendix B which also covers special designated walking and biking trails in Paris. As for pedestrian safety, walking the streets of Paris calls for the same kind of common sense precautions one would exercise in most urban centers. We have never been robbed, but we know several people who have been. Police patrols in the areas where we have rented have been altogether adequate, though there were fewer uniforms evident in the tenth. Wearing furs, jewelry and flashy clothes, especially in poorly lit neighborhoods off the beaten track, is an invitation to thieves. Appendix B lists telephone numbers for police and other emergency situations.

BRIDGES AND QUAIS

The different quais, or paved embankments, along the river between the bridges on both La Cité and Ile St-Louis and the opposite shores provide not only dramatic vistas of the river and city but also, with their sidewalk boutiques, a constant diversion for the stroller. Each quai derives its own personality from its surroundings—adjoining buildings, monuments, and connecting streets. The *bouquinistes* (second-hand book-sellers) on each quai tend to specialize in certain kinds of merchandise, various categories of used books, maps, stamps, engravings, posters and other objects appealing to collectors and tourists. Thus, a student looking for a cheap edition of one of the classics will go to the Quai St-Michel near the Petit Pont, one of four quais on the left bank. Stops for two major Metro lines and the Blue Line and Yellow Lines of the RER make Quai St-Michel one of the busiest transportation hubs in Paris. Another four quais stretch along the right bank opposite La Cité. On the perimeter of the island itself a ring of quais are delightful pedestrian routes.

Le Petit Pont is believed to be on the site of the first wooden bridge built in Gallo-Roman times at the closest point between the left-bank mainland and the island. In 1185 Bishop Maurice de Sully, builder of Notre-Dame, oversaw construction of the first stone bridge here. Later bridges were destroyed eleven times by floods or fire before the present bridge was built in 1853. A walk east from the Petit Pont along the Quai de Montebello on the left bank provides a fine view of the cathedral, its spectacular flying buttresses, and the surrounding park. Nearby is the Square René Viviani, a secluded enclosure surrounding the church of St-Julien-le-Pauvre and site of the oldest tree in Paris, an acacia planted around 1680. From here the Pont au Double leads to the front of the cathedral.

The next bridge, the Pont de L'Archeveché, links the cathedral grounds and the Square Jean XXIII, a space once occupied by ancient houses and small chapels that, until the beginning of the nineteenth century, obstructed the view of the towering walls of Notre-Dame. Next to the Square Jean XXIII, on the north side of the cathedral, runs the rue du Cloître, now cluttered with souvenir shops. To avoid these you can walk around the perimeter of the island or through the Ancien Cloître.

HÔTEL DE VILLE

Some of the few remaining private residences on La Cité line the Quai aux Fleurs. It follows the curve of the outer perimeter and leads to the Pont d'Arcole over the Seine and to the Quai de Gesvres on the right bank. This bridge offers the closest approach to the Hôtel de Ville, the imposing City Hall of Paris, which houses the offices of the Mayor and city government. The present building, a neo-Renaissance reconstruction built from 1874 to 1882 replaced an older structure which had been destroyed by fire in the bloody uprising of the Commune in 1871. On the walls of the present building niches shelter statues of 146 historic figures. The city of Paris has been governed from this site for over seven centuries, since the days when Saint Louis entrusted limited municipal administration to a select group of the powerful *marchands de l'eau*, the association of mariners who controlled navigation on the Seine.

Public hangings once took place on the square facing the Hôtel de Ville, while sorcerers and heretics met death here by burning at the stake. The town hall figured prominently in the Revolution. It was taken over by the *sans culottes* (the people's arm of the Revolution, literally "without trousers") after the storming of the Bastille and held by the revolutionaries until the end of the Terror. Robespierre received refuge here on the night before he was sent to the Conciergerie for execution on July 27, 1794, (9 Thermidor on the Revolutionary calendar.)

Until 1830 the square was named Place de Grève, and unemployed workers habitually convened here—hence the French word for labor strike, *grève*. Today the Place de l'Hôtel de Ville is the site for celebrating many popular holidays including the annual Feast of St. Jean featuring a twenty-meter-high bonfire. Panels along the walls of the Metro station here depict the riots, fires and other historic events that occurred on this site.

The Pont Notre-Dame, directly across La Cité from Le Petit Pont, was the first officially named bridge in Paris. After it collapsed in 1499, a new bridge, lined on either side with identical houses, became the preferred route for royal processions from the south into Paris.

Today the Pont Notre-Dame is the bridge closest to the Marché aux Fleurs, one of the city's several popular flower markets providing a colorful contrast to the rather drab municipal buildings surrounding it. Here on every day except Sunday dozens of stalls offer a huge choice of plants and cut flowers. On Sundays caged birds and other pets of all kinds make for a quite different but equally colorful marketplace.

Like the Pont Notre-Dame, the next bridge down-river, the Pont au Change leads to the Place du Châtelet named for the castle once guarding access to the bridge. A fountain in the Place du Châtelet commemorates Napoleon's victories. Two large theaters face this square, the Théâtre Musical de Paris and the Théâtre de Ville. Metro stops Châtelet and Châtelet Les Halles, each with connections to all parts of Paris, are also here. Because the latter is said to be the largest subway and a preferred site for pickpockets, we try to avoid it! The Metro line we use most, the east-west route Château de Vincennes-La Défense, stops at both Hôtel de Ville and Châtelet. This was the first line built in the Metro system.

A Glamorous Evening in the Haute Couture District

On our second night we took the Metro to meet Sylvie for a cocktail at the Crillon on Place de la Concorde. This world-famous luxury hotel has recently begun a once-a-month series of Sunday afternoon concerts in the splendid rooms overlooking the Place. The Crillon is within our ambit only on special occasions, but it was a convenient meeting place that evening. After cocktails we headed for the fashionable rue Faubourg St-Honoré, the site that evening of an elegant street party. Automobile traffic was diverted, pedestrians swarmed the sidewalks and street, and the high-fashion couturiers were hosting champagne parties for their customers. The theme of the evening, Napoleon and the Empire, was dramatically captured by the Hermès store. The Emperor was featured astride its rooftop equine statue while other life-like horses sporting brilliant Hermès designs peered out of all the upper story windows.

Sylvie had invitations to several couturiers' open houses including Hanae Mori and Balmain, where we dropped in to join the other guests, all turned out in the height of fashion, in consuming champagne and canapés. We then mingled with the throng in the street. An acrobatic Napoleon performed on a high-wire strung across the street. Mme. Chirac, wife of the then-mayor of Paris, led a marching band sporting brilliant Empire-period uniforms. As these festivities  were winding down, we hopped on the Metro to Sylvie's stop on rue du Bac and dined quietly in one of her neighborhood restaurants.

Among the great boons of our friendship with Sylvie is the gift-exchange custom she and Suzanne have developed. Tremendous care goes into the year-long process of selecting just the right items. In an early exchange Sylvie gave Suzanne a couple of exquisite scarves cut in the huge squares so popular with chic Parisians. At first it was quite a challenge for S. to figure out how to wear them. As one American observer of French fashion has said, there must be a required course in scarf-tying for all French schoolgirls which they must pass before graduation. Now Suzanne, with a little help from Sylvie but no formal course, has mastered the art of the scarf and wears these treasures practically with Parisian flair.

LEFT BANK ARTISTS IN A MULTIPLE VERNISSAGE

The next day was typical of our routine in Paris. As usual, after breakfast and a hefty intake of calories I felt the need for exercise and embarked on a walk along the river taking my sketch pad and camera. S. is a serious shopper skilled in tracking down bargains. On this day she scoured the rue St. Honoré almost from one end to another winding up at Mendès, (65 rue Montmartre) the off-price Yves St. Laurent. While it seems increasingly difficult to pick up bargains in Paris, she almost always finds something distinctively Parisian at a reasonable price.

For lunch we had selected a restaurant in the Marais on the Place des Vosges recommended in our apartment's guest book by previous renters. It turned out to be a crowded brasserie, and the best thing about it on that occasion was the low tab. (We changed our minds altogether on recently lunching at this always popular spot, Ma Bourgogne, where the hordes of sidewalk diners can enjoy the spectacle of the passers-by and the acrobatic waiters weaving through the confusion.)

After lunch we went to the Picasso Museum in the lovely Hôtel Salé, a restored hôtel particulier ideally suited for display of this artist's work. Though we have visited all the important collections of Picasso's work in Provence and elsewhere, for some reason Suzanne has never become much of a Picasso fan and had visited the museum once before, so we breezed through this collection in record time, then home for a nap.

That evening Sylvie again took us in tow, this time to an extravaganza of gallery openings in the St-Germain-des-Prés area, a hub of the artistic avant-garde. The entire area was swarming with gaudily garbed artists, and somewhat more conventionally attired collectors, art critics and the curious public. We threaded our way through the crowds into as many galleries as we could, winding up at one featuring *les trucs en fer* (iron-work gizmos) to which Sylvie had been invited. Among the weird and wonderful objects vying for attention, we thought the most intriguing was a stove in the shape of a baboon with the oven door in its belly. And yes, it was a working appliance!

A UNISEX COIFFEUR, THE PANTHÉON, AND TWO RESTAURANTS

We crammed a lot into our next to last day of that week. First was a visit to a His and Hers Coiffeur (Coiffeuse?) we had spotted the day before on the Boulevard St-Germain. What is now commonplace was for us in 1989 a novel experience—sitting in barber chairs across the aisle from each other and jabbering away with our barber/hair-dressers who were tending our locks.

After this venture, S. went window-shopping in favorite shops nearby while I went to what one unfriendly critic had called a "yard-sale" of objects salvaged from Versailles during the course of its extensive restoration. The exhibition, a mixed bag of great to not-so-great artworks and furnishings, took place in the Panthéon.

The area was familiar to me since we had once stayed in the little Hôtel Panthéon facing this famous landmark. Originally the church was intended as a shrine to house the relics of St. Geneviève, the patron

Saint of Paris who saved the city from the advancing Huns in 451. Parisians were fleeing in panic until Geneviève assured them that God would protect the city and the Huns shifted their attack to Orléans. Converted after the Revolution to secular uses, the Panthéon now is a lay temple where illustrious French heroes such as Rousseau, Voltaire, Victor Hugo, and Marie Curie are buried.

That night we dined with other Parisian friends at Le Vieux Bistro in the Ancien Cloître near our apartment. Situated just opposite the cathedral, this intimate spot personifies the bistro look of a bygone era with its unassuming decor and casual atmosphere. Happily, it seems to be unnoticed by the hordes of tourists passing by its doors but well attended by Parisian habitués. Its menu, like that of many older bistros make no pretensions to the *avant garde*. On the recommendation of our friends we ordered some of their favorite dishes including fresh *raie* (skate) with mustard sauce, a chicken/mushroom casserole and *crème brulée*. Our friends tipped us to the fact that this is one of the few Parisian restaurants open on Sundays. The relaxed dinner and the good company made for a perfect final night on La Cité.

Our Second Stay on La Cité

$\mathcal{I}$t was early in November of the following year when we again took the apartment on La Cité for a week. This time the moving in was a lot easier than the previous year; we knew our way around and were well prepared for the climb up the four flights. For our first shopping expedition we made a bee line to Ile St-Louis. The gridlike simplicity of this island's street layout makes it easy to navigate and impossible to lose one's way. The same cannot be said for the sometimes bewildering maze of narrow streets in other old quarters of central Paris.

If in your wandering you should become lost, and losing oneself should be regarded more as adventure than cause for panic, help is close at hand in the form of friendly police stationed at busy intersections. They usually carry street maps which they use to guide you in the right direction.

Ile St-Louis real estate includes some of the most expensive and sought-after properties in Paris; the *mètre carré* (square foot) rate is the highest in the city. The food shops cater to a sophisticated, well-heeled clientele. We had fun checking out all of these establishments, the specialty food shops, the wine shops and the few small grocery stores. And, of course, we joined the long line at the sorbet emporium, Bertillon, world famous for its many flavors of delicious *glaces*. An unusual measure of the success of this old family-owned establishment is the fact that it closes down for vacation during August when it could enjoy boom sales to the invading tourists. Our first shopping expedition on

Ile St-Louis was probably what inspired us to look for a future rental in what later became our favorite location.

MAISON FOURNAISE IN CHATOU

Shortly before leaving the States we had read about the opening of the restored restaurant, Maison Fournaise, on the island of Chatou west of Paris. Best known as the site of Auguste Renoir's famous painting, *Luncheon of the Boating Party*, the restaurant and the surrounding area had fallen into decay around the turn of the last century and ceased to be the fashionable retreat for the Parisian art world. The apogee of chic for Chatou occurred toward the end of the Second Empire with a visit from Napoleon III and Empress Eugénie. They wanted to see what attracted so many of the Parisian artistic illuminati including not only Renoir but also Guy de Maupassant, Jacques Offenbach, Edgar Degas, Ivan Turgenev, Claude Monet, and Gustave Caillebotte to name only the most renowned.

The Maison Fournaise was one of quite a few similar *guingettes* (the word derives from the cheap, sour wines produced by early Parisian vineyards) down-river from Paris along the Seine and clustered particularly at Chatou. Here Parisians could come by train, hurtling at thirty-one miles-per-hour, to escape the city and enjoy boating, swimming, country dining, and romancing in pastoral settings. Now restored and preserved as a national monument, Maison Fournaise recaptures a way of life otherwise lost to the ravages of "progress." By far the best way to visualize that special moment of history is to gaze upon Renoir's painting.

Now the cornerstone of the Phillips Collection in Washington, D.C., the painting was the featured work in the museum's 1996 exhibition of Impressionists on the Seine. Duncan Phillips had acquired the painting in 1923 for the highest price ever brought by a Renoir until then, $125,000.

Renoir began the painting in 1880 and labored over it until he had successfully captured the likenesses of the fourteen friends assembled for this event. They included a diverse array ranging from Baron Raoul Barbier, who volunteered to help Renoir assemble all the guests to sit for the painting, to the restaurant owner and even to the demimonde, represented by a prostitute and two actresses. Each of the fourteen had close bonds to Renoir (one was to become his wife five years after posing in the painting) and each were typical examples of the people who made Maison Fournaise and Chatou so popular. Renoir reworked his canvas many times as his models came and went and his ideas of composition changed. He was always frustrated by the difficulty of finishing the painting. Upon completion it won instant acclaim, but would Renoir have been able to forecast the universal appeal of this painting over one hundred years later?

Visiting Chatou today is the closest one can come to recapturing this enchanting epoch. On a sparkling sunny Sunday morning, when many Parisians start off for a leisurely lunch, we made the trip on the RER line A1 from Châtelet les Halles. At the Maison Fournaise restaurant every table was occupied by families—grandparents, parents and children, all in their Sunday best. The adults talked animatedly and smoked continually; the regulation requiring nonsmoking areas in restaurants had yet to go into effect. The children were mostly quiet and on their best behavior. These family groups seemed to fit timelessly into the picture and, despite their modern dress, helped recreate a sense of the past in the present.

The architectural renovation has faithfully preserved the atmosphere prevailing at the time of *Luncheon of the Boating Party.* Diners still use the covered terrace as well as an inside room decorated with murals capturing a long-forgotten era of Parisian political life. We enjoyed three of the *specialités de la maison, a terrine de lapin* (rabbit pâté), a chicken dish with olives, carrots and other vegetables, and a crème brulée all based on recipes of Alphonsine Fournaise, the wife of the original proprietor. Returning to our apartment in the late afternoon, we enjoyed a relaxed dinner at home featuring Suzanne's version of roast chicken.

One of her first purchases on moving into an apartment is always a chicken, preferably one of the readily available precooked birds, which, after the initial meal, reappears in various guises including chicken salad. The taste of French chickens puts the average American or British chicken to shame. Most birds sold in French shops are free-range—succulent and very tasty. Non-French shoppers may be a bit thrown off by seeing the head and feet still attached to many but not all of the chickens. My not-too-squeamish wife has on occasion coped with the undressed birds.

After the bird's first appearance at

the table S. often makes a simple *gratin* of chicken using a cream sauce and adding whatever cheese happens to be on hand in the fridge (camembert, cantal, brie and jarlsberg work especially well.) Mix cut up chicken with this sauce in a shallow-baking dish, sprinkle with a little grated cheese, place under the broiler until browned, and *voilà* chicken gratin.

TASTING PARIS—IN THE APARTMENT OR ON THE TOWN?

Why would anyone in their right mind decide to eat in their apartment when Paris offers such ready access to so many kinds of cuisine in restaurants at all price ranges? After all, time in Paris is precious and there is so much to do and see that even a serious chef might resent time spent cooking in an apartment kitchen. Furthermore, most rental apartments, except those that are sometimes used by their owners, have only minimal equipment. A small fridge, two burners, a microwave oven, and a coffee maker have been all we've had in several of our apartments. But we get by just fine without more kitchen gadgetry.

The main benefit of a kitchen in a Paris apartment is breakfast. We much prefer breakfasting at home to going out. What used to be the typical Continental Breakfast (the American or British style breakfast is gaining wider acceptance in tourist-oriented Paris) seems somewhat skimpy to us, though we adore the croissants or baguettes, which must be acquired fresh each morning from the best of the local *boulangeries*. I am always deputized to pick up these items while out to buy a newspaper. When I return, S. has prepared the rest of breakfast—fresh orange juice or other fruit, eggs or cereal and always *strong* coffee. Incidentally, bacon as we know it is sold as *poitrine fumée*.

We also enjoy an occasional lunch or dinner at home. There are many good reasons for apartment renters to make use of their kitchens for these meals. Economy is one, but the most important is that cooking at home gives you the excuse to shop in the Parisian fashion—visiting the many different types of specialty shops, the open air markets, (Paris boasts no less than fifty of them, and they are all listed in *Paris Inside Out,* pp. 339-342, See Appendix C) and the *supermarchés* for kitchen staples and other household needs. To miss out on food shopping in Paris is to miss an essential aspect of life of the city.

SOME TIPS ON LOCAL SHOPPING

Apartment dwellers should be prepared to adapt their daily routine to the rhythm of Parisian life. The adjustment can be greatly eased by learning about the hours of store openings and closings noted in the checklist at Appendix B. As indicated there, however, these hours sometimes change to accommodate customers, and you will need to discover for yourself the schedules of your neighborhood shopkeepers.

Your pleasure in shopping will be greatly enhanced if you adhere to the ritual exchange of greetings and store manners. The shopkeeper will open with *"Bonjour Monsieur or Madame"* to which you reply with a similar greeting. The familiar use of first names is *not* part of the ritual. Conversational exchanges about the weather, neighborhood news or other items are welcome provided they do not interfere with transacting business on the part of other customers. The shopkeeper will bid you a friendly goodbye and thank you for your purchase as you leave, and you should respond in kind. Do not try to break through the wall of reserve unless over a long duration you have established some unusual connection or relationship with the store owners. Then you can consider that you are truly integrated into Parisian life.

MEALS AT HOME

By taking some meals at home, of course, you can realize some real cost-savings, although it is possible to dine well in restaurants at fairly modest prices. The temptation is always to consume too much rich restaurant fare, and simpler home-cooked meals are often a welcome change, especially if you are tired from sight-seeing, museum-hopping, and shopping. Relaxing with lunch or dinner at home is a good way of pacing your visit. A tip for the economy-minded; taking lunch at a restaurant and dinner at home is the less costly way to go, since the same or equivalent meal usually costs a great deal more in the evening than in midday.

Simple home meals of salad, cheese, sausage, bread, fruit, and wine are easy to prepare and delicious to eat. Also, as noted above, we are strong advocates of the roasted chicken acquired either uncooked from the local *boucherie* or pre-roasted from a *traiteur* (delicatessen or take-out shop.) Traiteurs in most neighborhoods offer prepared food of all kinds, sometimes including baked goods and pastries. Selections include tarts and quiches, salads, terrines, pâtés, dozens of cheeses, and delicious desserts. The quality of traiteur offerings varies tremendously as does that of neighborhood bakeries and pastry shops.

Markets and shops selling produce provide all sorts of fresh vegetables and fruits at prices comparing favorably with American stores. Such special items as *mâche*, endive, and *haricots verts* (thin filet string beans) often going for a premium in the states are pretty reasonable in Paris. Other products S. cherishes include unsalted butter, veal (easily and quickly cooked), Cavallon melons in summer, and Italia (muscat) grapes.

If price is not a concern, the place to go for delicacies to take home is the gourmet emporium Fauchon or its nearby competitor Hédiard, both near the Madeleine. Both of these establishments date back to the middle of the nineteenth century, both qualify as *épiceries de luxe*, and both have loyal patrons. Fauchon has several branches in or near Paris. The Fauchon restaurant and cafeteria are among our favorite dining spots. Some of Suzanne's suggestions for pick-up lunches, sandwiches, snacks, picnics, or dining in the apartment follow.

PICK-UP LUNCHES, SANDWICH COMBINATIONS, APPETIZERS AND PICNICS

Pick-up lunches and sandwiches, almost as popular in Paris as in the U.S., can be made from all kinds of cheeses, pâtés, *terrines*, sausages, prosciutto-like ham cut thin, *tapenade* (an olive and anchovie based paste) and the other spreads available at traiteurs. The variety of breads for sandwich-making is mind-boggling. In addition to the well-known baguettes and croissants, the *boulangeries* (bakeries) offer such products as walnut bread, olive bread, rye bread with raisins, *herbes de Provence* breads, and *boules de campagne*, round loaves of brown country-style bread.

Not long ago the production and supply of bread became an issue of great national concern. Authorities were seriously worried about a dramatic fall-off of bread consumption, to the point where many independent bakers were going out of business, while frozen bread dough and even baguettes were being mass produced in great volume. A 1993 decree stipulated that only bread made at the point of sale could be advertised as *pain maison* (home-made bread.) Government intervention staved off the demise of one of France's most treasured gastronomic icons, and today boulangeries are again producing the quality and variety of breads for which they have long been known. (Chalk up a win for the regulators!)

A standard picnic fare is the quintessentially French toasted ham and cheese sandwich, the *Croque Monsieur*, an item that probably originated around the turn of the century and now flourishes all over France. Easily obtainable in the take-out shops abounding in Paris, it can also be made very simply in the apartment taking advantage of the distinctly Parisian cheeses and hams. Restaurateurs have concocted countless variations on this simple recipe including vegetarian versions and those with poached eggs on top.

One of the special pleasures of Paris food shopping is the ready availability of delicious appetizer treats at neighborhood traiteurs. If you are having guests before going out to dinner or perhaps you yourselves want to have a cocktail at home before you venture out, you walk only a few steps to a traiteur to select from a tantalizing selection of delicacies or as the French so aptly call them *amuse-gueules* (literally tickle the mouth). The variety of choices is staggering. Pâtés range far and wide from the traditional *foie* or liver based pastes to the forestier varieties featuring forest mushrooms and herbs to types for the liver-averse consumer such as smoked ham, vegetable, or fish pâtés. An endless range of other ingredients encompasses cream, eggs, spices, truffles; and the mix is often marinated in wine or brandy.

The pâtés are finely ground, frequently served *en croute* (in crusts) and elegantly garnished so that when sliced they reveal a pattern of textured ingredients beneath a clear gelatin or other topping. Their country cousins the terrines, are less finely ground and never served in crust. Terrines boast coarser chunks and sometimes strips of duck, chicken, goose, or pork with a texture comparable to the Anglo/American meat loaf. In French usage, however, the distinction between the two types of dishes is blurred almost to the vanishing point. Mustard, particularly Dijon, suits either pâtés or terrines.

Cornichons or gherkins are also natural mates of either dish and come in a mindboggling variety, all of which you should subject to your own taste test. Also try out the olives which come in even more varieties than cornichons. Traiteurs take great pride in their house specialties. Some offer little cheese puffs, or brochettes of scallops or chicken. The embarrassment of riches is summed up in the French expression *"Les choix ne manquent pas."*

SALAD IMPROVISATIONS

Infinite opportunities for improvising are waiting in the produce stalls of Parisian neighborhood markets. Shopping these markets is an aesthetic opportunity to exercise all the senses. Feast your eyes on huge

artfully constructed displays of colorful fruits
and vegetables, inhale the aromas ranging
from subtle to overwhelming as you pass
from one area to another, relish the feel
of the items you touch in deciding
what to purchase, and the taste
of some of those items after
you have made your selec-
tion. Not only will you find
most of your favorite standbys, but there are
also many varieties of lettuces, great quantities
of mâche, and greens, abundant *haricots verts*,
and other vegetable ingredients to toss in just for fun. Some markets
carry packaged celery root already julienned. One can always find
cooked beets *(betterave)* which the French love to feature in salads.

Goat cheeses seem to lend themselves particularly well to salads.
(See cheeses below) In Paris you will never run out of different varieties. Vinaigrette dressings come ready mixed or you can follow your
own recipe. Some apartment rental agencies provide kits of basic
kitchen staples including the makings for salad dressings. Relatively
few rental apartments provide other staples in their kitchens.

MUSSELS—MOULES MARINIÈRES OR MOUCLADE

We have found the *moules* or mussels in France to be even more flavorful than those in the U.S. When you are in France try them in
restaurants, or, if possible, cook them yourself—and see if you agree.

Preparation

Mussels should be washed in cold water one or more times to remove
any sand, and scrubbed if the shells look dirty or covered with seaweed.
Also the "beards" should be pulled away or snipped. This step should
not be done in advance of cooking lest it cause some of the mussels to
die. (These instructions apply particularly to mussels harvested from the
wild, but nowadays more and more mussels sold commercially have
been farmed, and these tend to need less pre-cooking preparation.)

Cooking instructions usually advise discarding any open mussels in
case they are no longer alive. However, some will close slowly if tapped
or pressed: others will resist and are clearly alive. Examine these closely and use your judgment. There are few if any dead ones among cul-
tivated mussels.

MOULES MARINIÈRES

2 quarts (about two pounds) mussels
1 cup dry white wine
1 clove garlic, minced
2 shallots, chopped
handful chopped parsley and/or other herbs you
    fancy
salt, freshly ground pepper

Place mussels and other ingredients in large pot. Cover and cook over medium-high heat for about six minutes, shaking or stirring occasionally until all mussels have opened. Discard any that have not opened. The mussels with their broth can be eaten at this point just as they are, soaking up the broth with bread. For a richer dish you can make a sauce.

To prepare the sauce first remove mussels from pot. Pour liquid into a saucepan through a sieve lined with dampened cheesecloth to remove any trace of sand. Stir in three tablespoons of soft butter mixed with one tablespoon of flour. Reduce by half stirring often (three to four minutes). Pour sauce over mussels served in soup plates. Garnish with parsley.

LA MOUCLADE (A REGIONAL SPECIALTY OF CHARENTE)

The dish above can be enhanced by the addition of one or more flavorful vegetables such as mushrooms (two or three), a small leek, fennel, or carrot, and some heavy cream. The vegetables, diced or julienned and sautéed in butter until tender, are then cooked along with the mussels and served in the sauce. But to avoid overcooking do not include them in the sauce reduction.

Add to the sauce three to four tablespoons heavy cream, a pinch of saffron, one teaspoon thyme and cook until the mixture begins to boil. Stir in reserved vegetables, which mingle with the cream to create a deliciously aromatic sauce. Serve in same manner as *moules marinières* with French bread to soak up sauce.

LEEK TARTE *serves 4-6*

Pastry for a 9" pie or tart pan
1 pound leeks
⅓ cup shallots, minced
½ stick butter
3 eggs
1 ⅓ cups heavy cream
⅔ cup milk
nutmeg, salt, pepper to taste

Lightly oil pie or tart pan; place pastry in pan, cover with foil and weigh down with pie weights or raw rice. To prevent pastry from shrinking first place it in refrigerator for forty minutes, then in freezer for twenty minutes. Bake at 400°F for 15 minutes. Remove foil and bake 10-15 minutes more. Pastry need not be browned at this point.

Cool on rack. Halve lengthwise the white and pale green part of leeks, wash carefully and cut into ¼" slices. In skillet over low heat sweat leeks with the minced shallots in the butter, covered with wax paper and a lid for 15 minutes or until leeks are soft. Drain and cool.

Whisk eggs, milk, cream and nutmeg, salt and pepper to taste. Spread leek mixture on bottom; pour custard over it. Bake in top of oven at 375°F for 20 or 25 minutes until custard has begun to set. Remove quiche from pan and cool 5 minutes on rack.

(If this seems too complicated or if the apartment kitchen isn't adequately equipped, take the easy way out. Buy a quiche at your local traiteur.)

I CAN'T BELIEVE IT'S TURNIPS *serves 2*

2 small turnips (about ½ pound)
⅓ cup good quality Parmesan
   cheese
2 ½ tablespoons butter, melted
¼ to ⅓ cup sour cream or crème
   fraiche
salt/pepper to taste

Peel turnips and slice thinly. Butter bottom of a small shallow baking or gratin dish. Lay turnip slices overlapping, to form a layer covering bottom of dish. Spoon half of the sour cream over layer of turnips, then one third of the cheese. Salt and freshly ground pepper to taste. Drizzle one third of the melted butter over all. Repeat, making two more layers, and using turnip slices to spread out the dollops of sour cream as you go. On top layer drizzle remaining butter and sprinkle liberally with Parmesan cheese. Place dish on a baking sheet in case of boil-over and bake in oven preheated to 350°F degrees for 20-25 minutes until top is nicely browned and bubbly.

CHOOSING AMONG FOUR HUNDRED CHEESES

General De Gaulle summed up the significance of the French love affair with *fromage* when he spoke of the impossibility of governing a country that had 246 different officially designated types of cheese.

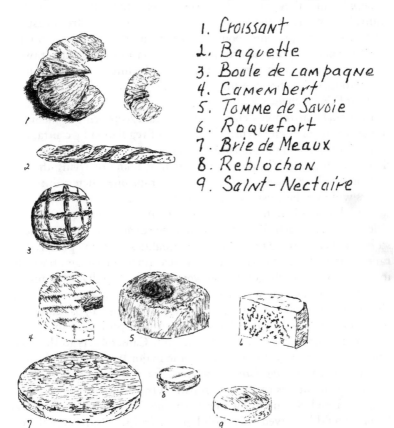

1. Croissant
2. Baguette
3. Boule de campagne
4. Camembert
5. Tomme de Savoie
6. Roquefort
7. Brie de Meaux
8. Reblochon
9. Saint-Nectaire

According to latest count by the powerful national association controlling cheese *appelations*, there are now over four hundred registered cheeses. The taste attributes of cheeses depend on three major factors; namely the animal source (whether cow, sheep, or goat), the grazing land, and the producer. France is blessed with ample herds of all three types of animal and good pasture land for each. Considering the consumer demand and the producer's interest in defining market niches for their products, it is no wonder that the number of cheese classifications keeps growing.

In addition to the recognized classifications there are countless varieties of cheeses produced all over France by small farmers or artisans who sell their products independently, often on the roadside at the farm source. These *fromages fermiers* or artisanal cheeses have become so popular that they can sell for seven to eight times the price of their equivalents made by the large producers. Cheese made from pasteurized milk now represents about eighty percent of French consumption while the non-pasteurized artisanal cheese consumption is about twenty percent. U.S. health regulations prevent the import of non-pasteurized products, so that consumers in America are unable to buy the choicest French cheeses.

In French gastronomy cheese has no rival except wine in the intensity of feeling of connoisseurs, the degree of regulation by central control authorities, and the pleasure enjoyed by consumers in shopping for their favorite brands and relishing them at home or trying them in restaurants. The cheese course in a restaurant often determines how diners will rate the cuisine of the restaurant.

A highly sophisticated code governs what cheeses to serve with specific wines, how each cheese type should be cut at the table, and how to store them to preserve their individual qualities. In many good restaurants waiters will advise you on cheese selections and suggest the order in which to taste each, going from *douce* to *fort*. Top flight restaurants will offer anywhere between a dozen and twenty-odd cheeses for their cheese course. These will range from the soft unaged goat cheeses to the solid Tommes and Beauforts of the Alpine provinces, to the ripe and gently flowing Bries, Reblochons and Camemberts to the blue-veined Roqueforts, just to mention some major types. The association controlling cheese *appelations* specifies, for example, that different types of goat cheeses can be accompanied by different types of wines ranging from light and dry whites to full-bodied reds, while *Tomme de Savoie* should be served only with light or fruity reds, *Bries* with reds ranging from light to full-bodied, and *Roquefort* only with full-bodied reds.

S. and I make no claims of cheese connoisseurship. We have come to know and like certain cheeses, which we buy in France and, when they're available, at home. She discriminates more than I do in her cheese choices. It might be said that I have never met a cheese I didn't like. For example, I am fond of both goat cheeses and the Roquefort family of blue cheeses, which are not on her list. Even I draw the line at some of the ripe and awful smelling types. Cheeses we do enjoy include the many types of Brie, Reblochon, Tomme de Savoie, Chaumes, Saint Nectaire, Saint André, and Port Salut. We especially enjoy cheese with red wine at the cocktail hour, a custom French cheese fanciers would frown on.

THE MARRIAGE OF WINE AND FOOD

A great reward of our annual visits to France over the past fourteen years has been learning about and sampling wines. The many dozens of wines we have tried have been a mere scratch on the surface of the incredible variety, and our palates, as in the case of cheeses, have not reached the rank of connoisseur. Like many other American wine drinkers, however, we have developed our own ideas about what we like and which wines go best with our favorite dishes.

Two shifts in oenology occurring since we started going to France have affected our own outlook on wines. First, we no longer feel rigidly bound by the old rule about serving white wine with fish and red wine with meat. That rule still makes good sense in most cases, but there are plenty of times when it can be broken, as the French have done for years. Perhaps it should be noted here that the proportion of red wine consumed by the French is far higher than white, especially in the south of France. In northern France, especially in areas close to Germany and the Rhine, white wine predominates. Likewise in the United States white wines continue to be more popular than red. Rather than being guided by color one should take account of how such factors as body, bouquet, and sweet-to-dry complexion will marry with a particular dish or meal.

Secondly, we happily support the comeback being made by rosé wine which has been out of fashion in the U.S. until recently. A bottle of rosé goes especially well with lunch, and we look for some of our favorites from Provence including the popular Tavel. Rosé has a special cachet in Paris because it is the wine produced by the Clos Montmartre, one of several small vineyards in the city and the one marking the official start of the national *vendange*, the grape harvest. The grapes from this vineyard, fermented in the cellars below the office of the Mayor of Paris, produce an annual yield of about 450 bottles. Long considered an almost undrinkable *guinguette*, the Montmartre wine has gained more acceptance in recent years. A problem with this vineyard from the beginning is that it faces a northern exposure. The jovial band of Montmartre bohemians who started it in 1934 had little concept of such practical matters as the proper exposure and slope of the land.

We have visited all of the major red wine producing areas in France and are leaning a bit more toward reds in wines we serve at home. I now am more likely to choose a red than a white wine at dinner time partly because I prefer the taste and partly because medical professionals seem to think there is a beneficial chemical in red wine. We shop around for best buys of French wines and find plenty of choices at reasonable prices comparing favorably with domestic wines. We like especially the Madiran wines from the southwest which we discovered in Gascony, the *Côte du Bourg* wines, among the lesser known Bordeaux, the famous reds of Saint Emilion, and the Gigondas wines of the Rhone Valley.

THE "BAD" MEAL

Before leaving this discussion of food let me comment on the conventional wisdom that "you can't have a bad meal in France." Experienced travelers to this world capital of fine cuisine know all too well the fallacy underlying this myth. Furthermore much of the ordinary fare offered in ordinary bistros, cafés, fast food joints and restaurants can be pretty awful—no better, if not worse, than what you might find in the United States or Britain. While many Parisians enjoy leisurely restaurant luncheons, one also sees hordes of busy working people lined up at run-of-the mill places for a hurried lunch, perhaps one advertised on the chalk billboard in the window pushing the *plat du jour* and other daily *spécialités*. Or they may be walking along while wolfing down a baguette or croissant sandwich, not necessarily fresh-baked. The scene could be New York, London, or any urban setting where fast food counteracts an atmosphere conducive to fine cuisine.

S. and I have had enough disappointing meals to know that it pays to choose restaurants very carefully, *not* on impulse because it "looks" cozy or charming. You don't need to limit yourself to places listed in the guides as there are plenty of good eating places not listed, often because they are too small. But if you care seriously about cuisine, look before you leap. Check out the menu and prices posted in the window, see how many other diners there are, don't hesitate to step inside for a sniff and look-around.

We learned a lesson the hard way in a little place on Ile St-Louis that we had passed on several occasions and from exterior appearances seemed to have plenty of "atmosphere." Once inside and seated at a table, however, the atmosphere turned out to be a state of rather filthy neglect and unsavory kitchen smells. Then we observed another danger signal: well into the dinner hour there were only two other couples seated. We ordered two of the evening specials, believing that to be the safest approach. But the slovenly Mme. La Patronne plopped down two plates of something unattractive and unappetizing. The concept of "presentation" seemed totally alien here.

While we were considering whether to skip on to a dessert we were enshrouded in a pall of Gaulloise cigarette smoke emanating from Madame's ashtray in her little booth near our table. We pointed to the offending cloud and asked if she could finish the cigarette elsewhere. But she only moved the ashtray a short distance to the other side of her perch. Meanwhile, a little terrier belonging to one of the other couples started yapping fiercely at the resident cat. His owners struggled without success to bring him under control. The idea of the simple but delicious dinner in the cozy restaurant vanished in the smoke and din. We paid the check, and, relieved but hungry, escaped into the night.

CHARTRES

Inspired by Henry Adams's masterpiece, *Mont St. Michel and Chartres*, which S. had given me for Christmas, we visited Chartres, taking a Paris-Vision tour bus from the rue de Rivoli. Paris-Vision is one of several companies operating tour buses in and around Paris (see check list in Appendix B.) We find such guided tours an inexpensive and enjoyable convenience especially for places outside of Paris. Henry Adams's classic, never out of print since its first publication in 1913, should be required reading for visits to any of the medieval cathedrals. At dinner the night before our Chartres excursion some friends had advised us that we should try to find an Englishman, Malcolm Miller, who is not only a well-known guide at the cathedral but also a widely recognized and extensively published authority on its history. On arriving in Chartres we entered the cathedral with our bus guide and the rest of our tour group. As we listened to our guide's rather routine talk, our ears caught the sound of a male voice speaking English with a British accent. It had to be Malcolm Miller, so we slipped away unobtrusively from our group and crept towards the rear of the little circle gathered around him.

His riveting discourse focused on a pair of stained-glass windows. Before long we realized that Miller's deep knowledge and respect for the cathedral did not inhibit him from taking a few jibes at the foibles and weaknesses of the sanctimonious bishops and priests who sought to memorialize themselves in the building. These same clergy were the ones who threatened eternal damnation to parishioners who failed to come for confession or, even worse, to support the building of the cathedral with both their money and their labor.

In describing the two windows Miller wove in fascinating details on the supreme position of the Virgin as inspiration for Chartres. The building and its windows were conceived as monuments to her, and her imagined requirements for design, color, and space. The needs of the worshipers other than a shelter from the elements and space to congregate were of secondary importance. The Virgin as Queen is depicted in various ways as very like the contemporary queens and nobles of France such as the Countess of Chartres, only the Virgin's tastes were finer.

From the first pair of windows we moved to the exterior of the cathedral where Miller spoke with feeling about the great rose window. The architect focused attention on this magnificent masterpiece, it is said, because the rose represented the symbol of the Virgin. With his talk on this window Miller concluded his tour. Even though our visit to Chartres was limited to these three windows while other more conventional tours took in the entire cathedral, we considered ourselves incredibly lucky to have been touring in the company of this knowledgeable and witty docent.

• • •

THE LOUVRE

During our 1989 stay on La Cité we had glimpsed the then-new and controversial I.M. Pei Pyramid at the Louvre but only from the outside. We had been very favorably impressed by the overall appearance of the new addition but discouraged by the long lines of people awaiting admission. The next year the Pyramid was working more effectively as the main entrance to the museum, though it can still become a bottleneck because many visitors fail to take advantage of the other points of entry. The initial flurry of controversy and criticism of the Pyramid by traditionalists was soon drowned out by the public's enthusiastic approval. Of the many monuments erected during the fourteen-year presidency of François Mitterand, the Pyramid has garnered by far the greatest public and critical acclaim. Dramatically placed in the middle of the Cour Napoléon, the huge glass structure covers the escalators leading down to the reception area (Hall Napoléon) on the Entresol where ticket booths and visitor amenities are located.

Having learned from experience that the most satisfactory way to visit the Louvre is to focus on some discrete aspect or area, we decided that this time we would concentrate on the building's history display next to the Hall Napoléon. This exhibit, which chronicles the evolution of the building over a period of eight centuries, features fascinating models and bas-relief plans of each stage of construction along with paintings, prints, and photos. The displays and descriptive labels lead us through the Louvre's transformation from a thirteenth century fortress down to the present palace. Viewers who find French history as difficult to keep straight as I do would double their appreciation of this display by advance reading of any good guidebook or history text. For a break between visits to different areas of the Louvre, the Entresol level also contains the vast new underground mall with shopping and restaurants. The shops offer a great variety of merchandise including clothing, garden supplies, hardware, and, of course, reproductions of the famous art works in the museum so that a serious shopper could spend many happy hours here. Of the several restaurants, Le Grand Louvre, directly below the Pyramid, offers the most memorable gastronomic experience with its specialties from the southwest of France, especially various dishes based on *foie gras*. Other classic cuisine specialties include pike dumplings and scallop ravioli.

On our most recent visit to the Louvre we lunched at the Café Marly in the Richelieu Wing. It has a long covered terrace (unheated and therefore usually deserted when the weather turns damp or cold) overlooking the Pyramid, as well as attractively decorated interior rooms. Its location and spectacular view of the Cour Napoléon together with a menu in the medium price range draws in many artists and art lovers. S. and I and the friend with whom we were lunching each took different dishes to share—a salad of mache and sliced chicken in a curry sauce, a terrine of steamed codfish, and scallops roasted in lemon butter.

TROUT WITH CAPERS *serves four*

Though not on the menu on the day of our visit to Café Marly, trout is every bit as popular in France as in the United States. One of Suzanne's favorite recipes for that most delicately flavored of all fish is an easy-does-it proposition.

4 small trout, heads and tails left on
flour seasoned with salt and pepper for dredging
5 tablespoons butter
4 mushrooms, minced
1 heaping tablespoon
   bread crumbs
juice of ½ lemon
1 tablespoon capers,
   drained

Dredge trout in seasoned flour and in heavy skillet brown on both sides in one tablespoon of butter per fish. Remove fish to hot platter. Add one tablespoon butter to skillet and sauté the mushrooms and breadcrumbs. Add lemon juice and capers. Stir briskly and pour over fish.

Père-Lachaise Cemetery

Although we had read quite a bit about this famous cemetery in the twentieth arrondissement, we had never been to see it. We figured that the best way to get there was bus #69 from Hôtel de Ville. The overcast sky set the proper mood for this visit to a site which, however interesting, is a city of the dead. The bus first traversed familiar arteries such as rue de Rivoli and Place de la Bastille then snaked through narrow winding streets in the eleventh arrondissement to the end of the line at Place Gambetta, a few steps away from the main entrance on Boulevard de Ménilmontant. From there the Avenue Principale leads into the central part of the cemetery. Rather than searching for the grave of any particular figure, we were seeking an overview of this landmark. The highly incongruous cast of France's historical figures ranges from the romantic duo of the twelfth century, Abélard and Heloise, to Oscar Wilde, Edith Piaf, and rock star Jim Morrison.

The story of how the remains of Abélard and Heloise fetched up in Père Lachaise is almost as extraordinary and convoluted as the story of their romance. Most readers will recall that Abélard was an extremely controversial theologian who attracted zealous student followers wherever he went. At one time this following was estimated at no less than ten thousand disciples. Always in trouble with the religious authorities, he was shifted from post to post and only rarely close to his beloved Heloise. During the period when he was banished to a remote monastery near the coast in Brittany they exchanged seven lengthy letters. Hers reveal the ardor of her love while agonizing over her sense of guilt and shame for the carnal sins committed with her beloved. His epistles focus mainly on spiritual matters and the discipline he recommends for the order of nuns to which Heloise belongs. The letters, while not gripping reading for most moderns, have been translated into many languages from the original Latin, and have gained the lovers immortality.

Their mortal remains, however, have endured numerous moves and indignities. At first they were entombed together in the abbey church founded by Abélard. English invaders destroyed the church, and one hundred years later they were reburied, but this time prudery dictated placing them on opposite sides of the abbey choir. The worst insult occurred when an enterprising owner of a private graveyard acquired their remains to be his Exhibit Number One. He even sold off pieces of bones as relics or souvenirs. When his cemetery closed, the bodies were moved to the old church of St-Germain-des-Prés where they were belatedly accorded a high mass. Their final destination was Père Lachaise. Here they were installed in a small chapel, now one of the principal tourist attractions.

Originally owned by the Jesuits who developed the area as a retreat and hospice for members of their order, this locale became a meeting place for high society during the time of Père Lachaise, Louis XIV's confessor. The land was acquired by the city of Paris and converted to a cemetery not long after the Revolution. In May 1871, the cemetery was the scene of the Paris Commune's last stand, and the 147 victims of that bloody encounter were buried en masse where they fell. In our rambling stroll Suzanne and I came across just two gravesites of famous figures, Colette and Delacroix. Only some of the most important Père Lachaise grave sites such as those of Frederic Chopin and Honoré de Balzac are indicated on the plan at the entrance gate.

The Crisis with the Car

One thing we are happy to do without in Paris is an automobile, an unnecessary contrivance for apartment dwellers in the city. But each year, either before or after our week in Paris, we rent a car for the time we spend in some part of provincial France. Usually we pick up and surrender our cars at De Gaulle or Orly airports. (The American offices of rental agencies are well prepared to arrange for rentals in France. If you want the car for more than three weeks, it pays to lease the vehicle. This means making a short term purchase of the vehicle which the rental agency buys back from you when you surrender the car. The savings can be substantial.)

After our stay in Paris in 1988 we took a house in the charming town of Bormes-les-Mimosas, one of several places designated as *villes fleuries*, (towns whose streets and walkways are lined with flowering plants), looking out from the top of a high hill over the Mediterranean. This was one of our most enjoyable rental experiences marred only by a hair-raising episode involving our rented Peugeot. We had picked up the car in the morning at the Marseilles airport and were taking a circuitous sightseeing route to Bormes. When the gas gauge indicated that we needed to fill up, we stopped at a Shell-BP station. I filled the tank with regular unleaded, which we had always used in our little cars. Twilight was giving way to dark as we picked up the autoroute toward Bormes. Very soon after leaving the gas station the motor began coughing and sputtering, and before long the car was slowing down despite my heavy foot on the accelerator. On a long curving hill, while we were hugging the right side designated for slow vehicles, the motor finally died. We were stranded in every motorist's nightmare—traffic zooming up the hill behind us and coming so close that I had to stand to the rear and wave people around.

Fortunately we were not far from one of the roadside trouble phones which are spaced at short intervals on all the autoroutes, each registering its location with the switchboard when you call in. Thus when S. reported our breakdown the operator knew just where we were and promised to send a truck in less than a half hour to push us into a nearby rest area. The operator also hazarded a guess that our problem might have stemmed from using the wrong kind of fuel.

The rescue truck pulled up behind us in about fifteen minutes, and pushed us into the rest area, where we were to await the arrival of another truck that had been summoned from the nearest town to take the car to a mechanic's garage.

In the relative security of the rest area we checked the manual of our Peugeot and found a one-line notice that it took diesel fuel. Later I found a small decal with the same message barely visible under the intake for the fuel hose. The agent who had rented the car to us had said nothing about this crucial requirement, but even so I cursed myself for not having the sense to check it out at the start. While we agonized about this foul-up the truck from the *garagiste* arrived with a driver and his helper. They hauled our car on to the flat-bed behind the truck, and we began a roundabout journey back to the town where I had made the big blunder. All the way we worried about how much damage had been done to the motor.

In the town we crept through narrow nondescript alleys to an open space in front of a dilapidated building, which seemed to lack the paraphernalia of a modern high-tech garage. Auto parts, tools, and tires were strewn about. As we climbed down from the truck's cab, we feared that we had wound up in a boot-strap operation. The garagiste tried without success to relieve our anxiety by cheerily repeating *"Pas de problème! Ce n'est pas grave!"* We wondered what could be a more serious problem. Then he told us that if we had made the reverse mistake, putting diesel fuel in a regular gas engine, the motor would have been totally wrecked. Somehow I was even more comforted when he later told us that even French drivers often use the wrong fuels, sometimes even in their own cars, thus contributing handsomely to his livelihood.

As the garagiste was collecting his tools, a loud honking from the alley announced the arrival of a rather fancy car from which bounced a well-dressed man and two youngsters. The driver introduced himself as Jean Pierre; the boy and girl were his niece and nephew. His exact connection to the garage and the garagiste was not evident, but he made a point of extolling the quality of the repair services to be performed. He also sought to entertain us with an account of the Sunday family dinner they had just consumed. He felt we needed to know about each of the numerous dishes, the wines served with them, and the liqueurs that followed.

Then came the tedious process of pumping out the gasoline, filling up with diesel and, then the really bad part, paying for everything including towing, all at Sunday rates. The bill came to about $160—not as horrendous as I'd feared or what it would have been if the reverse mistake had been made.

The episode ended when bon-vivant Jean Pierre urged us to come inside the garage where, on top of an old oil drum, five glasses of kir were neatly arranged for our send-off. The garagiste, his wife, his helper, Jean Pierre, Suzanne, and I toasted each other, we savoring the restorative powers of the kir. We thanked them for rescuing us, and after shaking hands all around, took directions for the next leg of the journey and drove off. The memory of the kir has almost, but not entirely, obliterated that of the events leading up to it. In subsequent years we have always carefully checked which type of fuel a rental car takes.

Rue des Petites Écuries

$\mathcal{I}$n search of an apartment in a different part of Paris and preferably one with fewer stairs than the one on La Cité, we contacted an alumnus of my college who frequently advertises Parisian rental apartments in the alumni magazine. He sent us literature and photographs of several apartments in which he has an interest, and we chose what was described as a studio duplex in the tenth arrondissement. This area, with which we were totally unfamiliar, lies roughly in the middle of the northern half of the city. The Gare de l'Est is its best-known landmark.

Even though the owner had warned us of the seediness of the neighborhood and the drab appearance of the ground floor entry, we were dismayed by our initial impressions. The rue des Petites Ecuries is a narrow and rather dingy street jammed with noisy automobiles and vans of the local businesses, mostly furriers. Known now as the Sentier quarter, the area is the center of wholesale trade for clothing materials and ready-made clothes. Our first challenge was mastering the complicated locks for two sets of doors and the elevator which served only the top two floors. Once in our apartment we realized that the "studio duplex" was actually a two level space with a ladder to a loft which held a second bed and some book shelves. However, the place was spotlessly clean, well-equipped with housekeeping necessities, and furnished with great imagination to make the most of the limited space. The intricate flower pattern of the coverlets on the bed, (green, violet and ocher,) was picked up in matching wallpaper on panels of kitchen cabinets and utility closet door to create an agreeable harmony. We liked what we saw and knew that our new digs would be just right once we settled in.

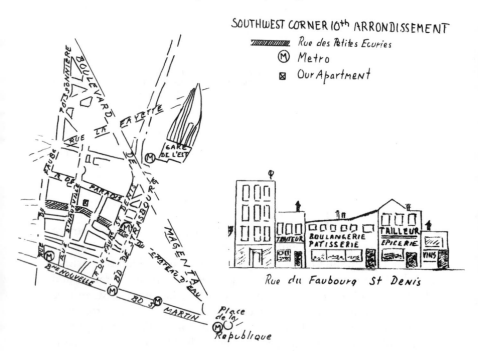

SOUTHWEST CORNER 10th ARRONDISSEMENT
Rue des Petites Ecuries
Ⓜ Metro
☒ Our Apartment

Rue du Faubourg St Denis

More than any other apartment we have rented, this one demonstrated that charming hideaways can be found behind unprepossessing exteriors and in unlikely neighborhoods. Our Parisian friends were amazed to hear that we were renting in this part of the city which, in their minds, was rife with prostitution and unsafe for pedestrians after dark. However, we found the people on the streets busily going about their tasks, many pushing garment racks or carts, with no time or inclination to make trouble. Though there were few police on patrol, never did we feel threatened, and once we learned our way around the neighborhood we were won over by its distinctive character. Graffitti on mail boxes by our front door proclaimed *"Vive les Arabes"* and *"Vive les immigrés."* The ethnic mix was heavily Arab, and during our week's stay we heard more Arabic than French spoken in the streets.

On our first day we lunched contentedly and inexpensively at Brasserie Flo (two forks in Red Michelin), a charming restaurant with handsome dark wainscoting, polished bronze, and huge urns of flowers evoking the Belle Epoque, when this part of Paris was a magnet for the *haut monde*. The restaurant is noted for shellfish, *foie gras*, *choucroute*, game, and *crème brulée*. After lunch we explored our new surroundings. The best find was an entire block on rue du Faubourg St. Denis lined on both sides with terrific produce stores, wine shops, and high-quality traiteurs where we could buy all sorts of wonderful delicatessen and bakery items at reasonable prices. We acquired a couple of delectable quiches, salad, pastries, and a bottle of wine for dinner at home while we planned our next day. The ready access to the traiteurs, and the absence of many good nearby restaurants led us to dine at home often while staying in this apartment. At one produce stall S. found packages of ready-julienned celery root handy for making a favorite salad.

CELERY ROOT REMOULADE

1 knob of celery root
½ cup mayonaise
Dijon mustard to taste
Optional-anchovies, capers, pickles, or herbs

A cold salad, used as a first course or side dish, is served much more frequently in Europe than in the U.S. Celery root (Celeriac, sometimes called celery knob) is about the size of a medium potato, with a taste like its cousin, celery. It enjoys a sunny spot in Suzanne's Washington garden.

Peel the celery knob and remove all traces of roots. Cut in quarters. Cutting julienne strips (or what chefs call "match sticks") by hand is a tedious, time-consuming chore, and food-processor julienne blades do a poor job. Several inexpensive mandolines with changeable blades will produce better strips with less effort.

An optional step is to dump the strips in boiling salted water to blanch quickly and remove the slight toughness. Drain dry in towel and let cool. Mix with remoulade sauce, (basically mayonaise with Dijon mustard added to taste.) Some people add anchovies, capers, pickles, or herbs, but S. prefers to skip anything that will overpower the flavor of the celery root.

If this dish were to become as popular in the U.S. or U.K. as it is in France, perhaps we'll begin to see packages of ready-julienned celery root in our produce sections.

The tenth arrondissement grew on us as we learned more of its colorful history and its distinctive architectural character. Toward the middle of the nineteenth century the main boulevards laid out by Baron Haussmann, the Boulevard des Italiens and the Boulevard Montmartre, the aptly called "Grands Boulevards" became the place for the fashionable set to drive their carriages past throngs of sidewalk observers taking their ease in straw-bottomed chairs. While many of the elegant houses once lining these boulevards have been lost to tasteless "face-lifting" and urban blight, a few reminders of the more glorious past remain. In particular, the huge triumphal arches celebrating military victories command attention at major street intersections.

In several walks along the Grands Boulevards we engaged in the architecture buff's search for the quintessentially Parisian street scene. Perhaps this is an idle quest since Paris has been a work in progress from the very beginning and no single site or collection of buildings can typify the many eras of the city's evolution.

While Haussmann's name is most commonly associated with the strict conformity to classical styles, height limitations and uniformity of facade designs, many building regulations existed long before Haussmann. Parisian architects had been indoctrinated in the classical style first in the Académie Royale d'Architecture (1671–1793) and later in the Ecole des Beaux Arts (1819 to the present). Only in the modern era has freedom of architectural expression flourished, but who can complain about the results of the rules governing the earlier periods? In our walks along the Grands Boulevards of the tenth we found that, despite too many cases of modernization not prevented by strict zoning regulations, the concept of Haussmann's grand design can still be appreciated in those landmarks that have survived.

Well worth a visit by all kinds of collectors is the Richelieu Drouot auction house near Boulevard Montmartre. Here at two o'clock every afternoon auctions are held in most of the sixteen auction rooms, and visitors can tour the auction galleries at other hours during the day. The laws governing auctions in France are notoriously archaic to the point where the prominent position of Paris in the art world is seriously jeopardized. Auctioneering is governed by a royal edict of 1556 confining the right to hold auctions to an exclusive monopoly. In an effort to overcome this antideluvian image the Drouot staged an auction open to Internet bidders in early 1997. The event attracted many more web surfers than the number of slots open for them, and much confusion resulted. Adapting today's information technology to an institution governed by sixteenth century regulation has become quite a challenge. Rue Drouot is also a favorite haunt of stamp collectors.

BOIS DE BOULOGNE AND BAGATELLE

One morning when we awoke to bright sunshine and blue sky we knew that the time had come for our first-ever visit to the Bois de Boulogne. The visit made us realize how much we had been missing. The park's scale (2,100 acres), the diversity of landscape styles from formal to natural, the range of recreational facilities and restaurants and, most of all, the sight of so many Parisians enjoying a Sunday outing made it a very happy experience for us. Even in late October the gardens were full of color, and S. was especially impressed by the vast areas of natural woods and open space reminiscent of English landscaper Capability Brown. The park's sports facilities include two popular race courses, equestrian stables, polo, tennis, boating, an amusement park for children, and miles of paths for runners, bikers, or walkers.

The Bois has undergone many changes since it was the private hunting preserve of the Merovingian kings of the fifth century. At various times the vast densely forested areas drew into hiding a variety of outlaws, poachers, refugees and the destitute. In a magnanimous gesture, Napoleon III presented the forest to the public and commissioned Baron Haussmann to landscape parts of the area. The winding paths, racecourse, ornamental lakes, and restaurants were built under the Baron's guidance.

The Bagatelle is a tranquil enclosed area within the Bois. Especially noteworthy are its gardens featuring water lilies, rhododendrons, roses, and irises. They surround a lovely complex consisting of two small chateaux facing a Cour d'Honneur. During the summer months two of the Bagatelle show-places built in the nineteenth century, the Trianon and the Orangerie, hold exhibitions of paintings and sculpture.

The little Bagatelle chateau was built in 1775 by the Count of Artois, brother of Louis XV, who accepted a challenge from Marie-Antoinette that he could not have the building constructed in a period of two months. Amazingly enough, the count won the bet, and today's visitor can enjoy the results of this royal whim.

For lunch we chose La Grande Cascade, (a second Michelin star awarded in 1997 plus four red forks), with full views of its lovely surroundings and not as *cher* as the nearby two star Pré Catalan. A waterfall constructed during the Haussmann period inspired the name of the restaurant, which was once the personal hunting lodge of Napoleon III. A curved glass verandah in the Art Deco style was installed in 1900, and the latest renovation in 1988 maintains the Rococco atmosphere of

the original. Our luncheon choices included two of the house specialties, a sautéed filet of turbot and a green apple tart, both of which lived
up to our high expectations.

Visitors to the Bois de Boulogne are warned against walking in the
area after dark because it is frequented by transvestites and other unsavory types. (See Appendix B for information on Paris parks.)

PARISIAN GREENERY

Its vast wooded areas together with all its sports amenities make the
Bois de Boulogne the second largest of the many Parisian parks after
the Bois de Vincennes on the opposite side of the city. In fact, no other
European capital matches Paris in the number and size of its green
spaces. S. and I regard this feature as one of the city's most alluring
aspects though it is unlikely to be the first thing most people think of
in connection with Paris. As I have already noted, S. is a serious gar-
dener, knowledgeable botanist and certified landscape designer. She
observes greenery with an expert's eye and helps me to learn about and
appreciate the *flora* we encounter.

A look at the city map shows parks scattered in nearly every quarter, and true Parisians treasure their favorite park as a vital resource. S.
and I have often thought that a long and blissful vacation could be
spent just visiting each of the parks. The short list in Appendix B
includes only some of the best known parks and gardens, but the
guidebooks in Appendix A should be consulted for more comprehensive and detailed coverage.

Aside from the parks where you can escape the man-made environment, Paris is blessed with more trees than any other city in Europe,
close to two hundred thousand according to some estimates. The city
government in a constant battle against the effects of pollution and disease maintains a computer file on each individual tree to monitor its
well-being. The effect of pollution on different species is studied in an
experimental greenhouse, and some thirty-five hundred new trees are
planted each year. While plane trees are the most common, the chest-
nuts still abound, and I relish the roasted *marrons* sold by street vendors
in the autumn.

Most of the great classical gardens of Paris were designed to surround royal palaces. The Tuilleries adjoining the Louvre was one of
the first royal gardens in Europe to be open to the public. Thanks to
successive city administrations the building of public parks and the

care for a green environment has never ceased and, indeed, enjoys more popular support than ever before.

VAUX-LE-VICOMTE

At the suggestion of the owner of our apartment, an architecture critic who had given us one of his articles on Vaux-le-Vicomte, we took a train from Gare de Lyon to the town of Melun, thirty-five miles southeast of Paris, and from there a taxi to this fabulous chateau— about an hour's trip altogether. The only other way of reaching Vaux aside from private automobile is one of the tour buses.

It would be hard to exaggerate the thrill of our first glimpse. Invariably compared with Versailles, Vaux often comes out the winner. The grandeur and vastness of Versailles are overwhelming, whereas the more human scale of Vaux can be grasped more easily. It is even possible to imagine actually living in Vaux, provided, of course, you had very deep pockets.

Such was the case with the builder and first master of Vaux, Nicolas Fouquet, the Supervisor of Finance under Louis XIV. But these same deep pockets led to Fouquet's undoing. At an extraordinary *fête* hosted by Fouquet in the King's honor, Louis saw and secretly envied the splendor of Vaux and its surroundings. Fouquet's arch rival, Jean-Baptiste Colbert, confirmed the King's lurking suspicions about the source of Fouquet's riches. It was clear that Fouquet could not have paid for Vaux without having dipped into the royal till. Less than three weeks after the fête the King ordered Fouquet's arrest. Following a prolonged trial Fouquet received a life sentence in one of Europe's harshest prisons and was never again able to enjoy the luxury of his palatial creation.

Although Fouquet is probably remembered most for his colossal misjudgment in trying to outshine the Roi Soleil, he deserves recognition for the superb sense of style and proportion exemplified by Vaux-le-Vicomte. Louis XIV lost little time in commanding the talents of those responsible for Vaux in the building of Versailles. Le Vau the architect, Le Brun the painter/decorator, and Le Nôtre the landscape designer—all were enlisted in the King's service at Versailles creating what would become known as the style of Louis XIV.

While the grounds surrounding Vaux have no bike paths or bike rental facilities like the ones we enjoy at Versailles, it has the great advantage of drawing smaller crowds, and you can take it in on one visit if you choose. You will find it hard to decide whether to concentrate on the chateau's elegant interior or the pale sandstone exterior that has remained virtually unaltered for more than three hundred years. What we enjoyed most was our leisurely walk through the vast gardens. Anyone lucky enough to visit Vaux-le-Vicomte today must be thankful that this treasure has survived revolutions and long periods of neglect, to be restored by the family of the present owners, who opened the property to the public in 1968.

After basking in the splendor of Vaux for several glorious hours we were all too soon jolted back into the real world. On the last leg of our return trip we found ourselves strap-hanging on a Metro jam-packed with families heading home from Sunday outings. We consoled ourselves by comparing our fate after Vaux with that of its unfortunate creator, Nicolas Fouquet. We, after all, were headed not for prison but for a quiet dinner in our cozy loft apartment.

A SIGHT-SEEING DAY IN PARIS

After a day away we spent the next day sightseeing in town. Our first stop was a widely acclaimed Grand Palais exhibition of Gericault, the nineteenth-century artist most often credited with breaking away from the classical into the romantic genre of painting. Large crowds were drawn by his vivid palette and the immense canvases depicting momentous events in French history. We timed our visit for the early lunch hour when museum lines usually dwindle. Thus we were able to avoid a long wait and to view the work of this master of heroics in relatively uncrowded galleries. We had made reservations for a late lunch at the Jules Verne (a star and four red forks in Michelin) on the second floor of the Eiffel Tower.

THE EIFFEL TOWER AND RESTAURANT JULES VERNE

Despite our qualms about dining in such a tourist magnet and the relatively pricey menu, we took the advice of several friends who had urged us to try this popular restaurant. The decor (stunning contemporary design with lots of gleaming metal, dark gray leather upholstery, black tables and table lamps,) ideally suited the site; service was good; and the luncheon menu offered fare that was well worth the relatively high tab. I chose steamed oysters *à la Chinoise* in a tomato sauce, while S. had a monkfish in a bed of braised endives.

Having enjoyed the Jules Verne experience at lunch we tried to reserve for a dinner there several years later and learned that the restaurant is booked many weeks into the future. Not until 1997 when I faxed five weeks in advance was I able to make a reservation. The evening was memorable in every way—Paris in its most magical aspect.

To assure maximum enjoyment of the Eiffel Tower experience at night (whether or not you are dining there) you should allow plenty of time, at least twenty minutes, to walk to it, preferably from the Trocadero metro stop. Go between the two wings of the Palais de Chaillot, down along the fabulous Trocadero Fountains and across the Seine on the Pont d'Iena. Even the most jaded world traveler will be enchanted by the spectacle of the tower's radiant skeleton rising above the night lights of Paris. Jules Verne patrons enjoy the luxury of a private elevator to their aerie, but the public can go to the level just below for the view.

The restaurant capitalizes fully on its monopoly of the view. Patrons should be prepared to accept that they are paying not just for the service and highly acclaimed fare but for a world-class location. Also be prepared to find yourself mostly in the company of other tourists. Bring your pocket book, swivel in your chair to gaze out in all directions, and enjoy!

Probably the best-known symbol of Paris, the Eiffel Tower has survived the initial intense opposition of some formidable critics and later threats of demolition and has eventually been accepted and treasured as a landmark. The original concession for the tower expired in 1909, twenty years after its erection, and the authorities had decided to tear it down. Only the fact that its antennae were considered essential to French radio-telegraphy saved it from demolition. Inevitably it is compared with latter-day monuments such as the Pei Pyramid which, incidentally, encountered far less opposition than the tower.

After our lunch at the Jules Verne, S. went shopping at one of her favorite little stores (unfortunately no longer in business) on the rue du Bac and found a great black-and-white houndstooth coat for about one-third the price it would have brought on Faubourg St. Honoré. I went exploring in Montmartre, which I had not visited in many years.

In retrospect, our week in the tenth arrondissement stands out as a wonderful period of discovery. We learned about a part of Paris little-known by most tourists; we enjoyed the ease and pleasure of dining at home on the delicacies of various local traiteurs; and we learned that behind the most unlikely facades can lie cozy and appealing retreats. Our shared love affair with Paris took on a new aspect. Most of our time in Paris before had been spent in the city's central parts with their ties to the distant past. In the tenth arrondissement our surroundings were more typical of the spreading metropolis and of the habitat of middle class Parisian workers.

Hôtel Duc de Saint Simon

With less than a week to spend in Paris in 1992 we decided to book a room in our favorite hotel, the Duc de Saint-Simon, rather than rent an apartment. Our appreciation of the Saint-Simon rose several notches after we learned the identity of a fellow guest. One day as I was approaching the Concierge desk in search of directions, I overheard the instantly recognizable throaty voice of the chic willowy woman ahead of me. With an impressive Parisian accent Lauren Bacall was chatting on friendliest terms with the receptionist and confirming arrangements for a second room in which to keep her luggage! (The St-Simon rooms *are* pretty small.) But if Lauren Bacall can deal with this minor inconvenience, certainly S. and I can cope, even in just one room, and enjoy the charm of this small hotel.

In her captivating memoir, *Now*, published in 1994, Lauren Bacall speaks fondly of Paris as "her heart's city," the Duc de Saint-Simon as her favorite hotel, the nearby bistros as the most congenial for enjoying every day rituals—breakfast (much more substantial than the Continental version) while reading the *Herald Tribune*, and people-watching in a neighborhood epitomizing the Left Bank's special cachet. In 1995 the French government, recognizing all that Lauren Bacall has done in films and writing to promote understanding of France, named her a Commander of the Order of Arts and Letters.

Though we thought we knew this neighborhood quite well, we discovered a delightful new (for us) restaurant, Le Petit Laurent, at 38 rue de Varenne (raised to three forks in the 1997 Michelin), just a couple of blocks from our hotel. We liked our new find so much that we returned

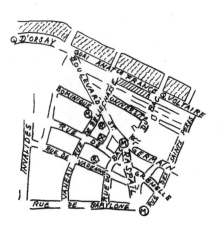

for a second visit—this time with our friend Sylvie who, though she lives nearby, had not known of it. Le Petit Laurent is our idea of just what a Parisian restaurant should be: small and intimate, simply but elegantly decorated, served by a good staff. We have dined there on each of our subsequent stays in Paris and have always been delighted with both the cuisine and the prices. Our judgment has been confirmed in subsequent glowing reports in two influential publications, *Gourmet* in the September 1997 issue, which notes that "its cosseting atmosphere and impeccable food would do a much grander establishment proud" and *Le Figaro* which in its October 20, 1996, issue praised the ambiance (elegant without ostentation) the cordiality of the service, the originality of the cuisine, and the unusual attitude of the chef and maitre d'hôtel who seem content to please their loyal clientele rather than clambering for notoriety. Let it be known that we discovered this little gem before the food Pooh Bahs awarded their laurels!

When it is on the menu, we always order Suzanne's favorite dessert, *Ile Flottante*, an old-fashioned standby which consistently shows up under various guises in many traditional Parisian restaurants. For the weight-conscious willing to forsake their diet on a special occasion here is the recipe she follows in her kitchen at home.

For Meringue
> 6 egg whites, (at room temperature)
> ¼ teaspoon cream of
>   tartar
> ¾ cups sugar
> pinch of salt
> ½ teaspoon vanilla or
>   almond extract

For Crème Anglaise
> 4 egg yolks
> 2 cups hot milk
> 4 tablespoons sugar

In this version the meringue is baked like a soufflé rather than laboriously poached by spoonfuls. The Crème Anglaise (custard sauce) can be made on the stove or in a microwave. Both the meringue and the sauce can be made a day or two ahead, and the sauce can be frozen.

The Meringue:

Heat oven to 250°F degrees. Oil bottom and sides of a 2-quart soufflé dish and dust with sugar. Beat egg whites at moderate speed until foamy; add cream of tartar and salt, increasing speed to high. Gradually add sugar. Flavor with vanilla or almond extract. Spread mixture in soufflé dish and bake 35–40 minutes or until soufflé has risen a few inches and a skewer poked to bottom comes out clean. If not, cook 3–4 minutes more. Allow to cool 30 minutes. Meringue will sink, but that's OK. Cover and refrigerate until ready to serve.

Crème Anglaise:

Conventional method:

Beat sugar into egg yolks. Heat milk to boiling, uncovered. Add gradually to yolks, beating constantly, until pale yellow. *Cook but do not boil* over low to medium heat, stirring with wooden spoon and watching carefully until custard starts to thicken. Beat faster and remove when custard coats back of spoon, and beat to stop cooking. Beat in 1 teaspoon unsalted butter (optional). Flavor with one or a combination of some of the following: 2 teaspoons vanilla extract, 1 tablespoon dark rum, 1 tablespoon Bourbon whisky, 2 tablespoon grated lemon zest, 1 tablespoon Grand Marnier.

Microwave Method

(Times refer to larger ovens (600–700 watts. Smaller ovens will need a few minutes more.) Beat sugar and yolks together. Bring milk almost to a boil in a 4-cup glass measure by cooking on high power 2 minutes. Gradually whisk milk into yolk mixture and return to glass measure. Cook on high power 45 seconds. Whisk 30 seconds. Microwave one minute longer and whisk again. If sauce is not yet thick enough, cook a little longer. Whisk in flavoring of choice. (Lumpy sauce can be rescued by straining or whirring in blender)

Optional Garnish:

Meringue may be dusted with pulverized nut brittle or crumbled macaroons or caramel drizzled over. Caramel: 1 cup sugar in ½ cup of water. Cover and bring to boil until amber in color. Turn off heat. Drizzle over meringue.

To Serve:

Place sauce in shallow bowl with scoops of meringue floating on top, or similarly in individual plates, garnish of choice on top.

GIVERNY AND MUSÉE D'ART AMERICAIN

We were lucky to catch the last day before the then new Museum of American Art in Giverny closed for the winter. An easy way to go is the A-1 express train to Vernon, fifty miles west of Paris, where you pick up a bus to Giverny. This was our third visit, so we focused more on the new museum than the house and garden.

In their European travels the wealthy American industrialist and art collector, the late Daniel Terra, and his wife, Judith, had observed that there are no important American paintings in any of the great museums of the continent. They dreamt of a modern facility to fill this gap in an appropriate setting in France. Giverny was chosen as the ideal site because many American Impressionists came here to study and paint with Monet and his friends. The Terra collection of American art includes many artists of the Impressionist school.

The Terras overcame numerous hurdles to bring their dream into reality. One of the toughest challenges was gaining local authorities' approval for the design of the museum building, which had to fit unobtrusively into the Giverny landscape. Numerous proposals were rejected, and prospects for the project were looking dim until an architect sitting next to Daniel Terra at a luncheon sketched his concept on a napkin. His design, as finally executed, fits perfectly into the terrain around it. Masterful landscaping of the grounds and the roof of the modern building have been widely acclaimed for their success in tying the structure to the land. Later in 1992, when the museum was to be opened, the Terras faced Parisian art circles skeptical of the worth and appeal of American artists, but skepticism has yielded to wide acceptance thanks to the high quality of subsequent exhibitions.

The permanent collection of some ninety works by artists including Hassam, Sargent, Cassatt, and Prendergast is still being augmented by gifts from the Terra Foundation. The exhibit spaces, mostly below ground to minimize the building's intrusion on the landscape, show these treasures at their best. On the day we were there we enjoyed lunching in the attractive restaurant looking out on the museum gardens.

Less than a block away from the Hôtel Duc de Saint Simon is another of our favorite restaurants, the Ferme St-Simon where we have dined frequently with Sylvie. This popular restaurant is likely to be booked up in advance by patrons who come from all parts of Paris for seasonal specialties. We do not understand why Michelin withdrew its one star in the 1997 edition. On one memorable evening as Sylvie's guest I recall ordering a rouget, a red mullet, floating on a *tapenade* sauce, a garnish made of olives and anchovies which we first discovered in Provence. S. ordered another popular Parisian fish, *daurade,* which was served in a bed of lightly steamed vegetables. I satisfied my chocoholic addiction with a bitter chocolate concoction while S. went for the *crème brulée.* Raspberries are almost always on the menu here when they are in season. Suzanne, who has a fabulous raspberry patch in her garden, belongs to the school that believes raspberries and chocolate have a special affinity. For an occasion that merits forgetting the calories, a recipe for one of her favorite desserts combining these two taste sensations follows:

CHOCOLATE RASPBERRY COMPOTE *serves 10*

½ pound bittersweet chocolate (not unsweetened)
2 cups heavy cream
2 cups raspberries
½ cup sugar
2 tablespoons orange liqueur
2 tablespoons bittersweet
  chocolate, grated for garnish

In double boiler melt chocolate in ½ cup cream, stirring. Let cool to room temperature, then whisk into the remaining cream. Chill thirty minutes in mixing bowl. Whip as you would plain cream, and fold in one cup raspberries. Spoon into compote glasses or dessert bowls and chill.

Process remaining raspberries until smooth, strain out seeds, and stir in sugar and orange liqueur. Top each compote with two tablespoons raspberry purée, and sprinkle with grated chocolate.

SOME TIPS ON RESTAURANT CONVENTIONS

First-time visitors to Paris may be interested in knowing how best to fit into the picture when they dine out. In fact, they will do well in following the universal code of good manners with minor adaptations to Parisian customs. In comparison with Americans, Parisians linger longer over their meals respecting all the effort that has gone into the preparation. They tend to begin their luncheons, and especially their dinners, at later hours than Americans, and chic Parisians never dine before eight o'clock at the very earliest unless they are heading for the theater. As one might expect, dress depends greatly on the formality of the restaurant or its rank in the star galaxy. Smart Parisians take their dress seriously, but, in the rapidly growing world of bistro dining, casual wear is "in," men's ties and jackets are mostly out. (When we were dining at the Jules Verne, I observed a group of American businessmen in tune with the current casual look draping their jackets on the backs of their chairs, suspenders in full display.)

Except in some still starchy high-ranking restaurants waiters have become more accepting of English speakers and able to communicate about menu choices. Waiters in our favorite restaurants cited in this text are very accommodating. Do not expect waiters to rush orders. For speed you have to go to *fastfood* places. Do not expect the waiter to introduce himself by his first name as you are being seated. Do not expect the waiter to bring your *addition* (the bill) until you have signaled for it.

French law requires that a fifteen percent service charge be included in your bill. *(Service compris* or *prix net)*. You do not need to leave a larger tip, but sometimes you may wish to leave a few coins by your plate if you've had particularly good service. It is an insult to the staff to leave the yellow *centime* coins. Big expense account spenders wishing to impress the management still give more substantial tips in notes to the Maitre d. It pays to phone for a reservation especially before dinner at one of the better restaurants. Credit cards are accepted almost everywhere, and many French restaurants have little computers which the waiter brings to the table. After inserting your card and punching in your bill you are instantly given a chit to sign and retain as a record. The gadget makes the waiter's job so much easier and saves so much time that one wonders why it has been so slow to catch on in America.

Ile St-Louis

$\mathcal{F}$or several years following our first rental on Ile de la Cité we had been hoping to find an apartment on Ile St-Louis. To our great delight we found one available through the same fellow who had rented us the apartment in the tenth arrondissement.

As we expected, it was comfortable, attractively furnished, and equipped with all the house-keeping essentials. With his rentals he also supplies his own helpful guides on neighborhood shops, restau-rants, and places of interest.

We had only scratched the surface of Ile St-Louis in our previous walks, and we knew little of its history. Unlike La Cité, which had been inhabited since ancient times, Ile St-Louis was undeveloped and used only for grazing cattle until the seventeenth century. Then two smaller islands were joined together to form the present eighteen-acre area. A consortium of speculators persuaded King Louis XIII to permit development on condition that they build the quais, streets, and two stone bridges to the mainland. Partly intimidated by the canons of Notre-Dame who held title to St-Louis, the King delayed payment to the developers, who consequently lost their shirts in the enterprise. But by the middle of the century Paris had acquired a piece of very desirable land that subsequently became an exclusive residential enclave.

The prime real estate facing the river was soon taken up by wealthy aristocrats, who built their imposing hôtels particuliers to take advantage of spectacular views. On the interior streets artisans and local merchants built shops and more modest residences. Although the island has seen many ups and downs over the years, it retains much of its original architectural character, and its residents still regard themselves as a special breed apart from what some still refer to as "the Continent." Island living seems almost always to promote a sense of territorial superiority.

Five bridges link the island to the mainland. The Pont Marie, which connects the middle of the island to the right bank, was named for Christophe Marie, the head of the consortium that developed the island. East of this bridge is the Quai d'Anjou, lined with the least-altered historic houses on the island. Three of the most notable houses are #27, Hôtel Nevers, where the Marquise de Lambert held her famous salon; #17, the Hôtel de Lauzun designed by Louis Le Vau for M. Gruyn, caterer to the Army, who did several turns in prison for embezzlement; and at the corner of Quai d'Anjou and rue St-Louis-en-L'Ile, the very grand Hôtel Lambert, also designed by Le Vau and decorated by Le Sueur.

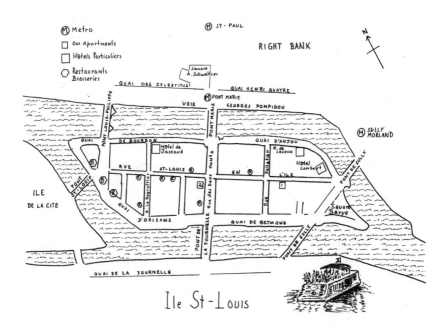

Ile St-Louis

The Hôtel Lambert typifies the radical changes in fortune that have beset Ile St-Louis residences over the years. Early in the nineteenth century the building became a mattress warehouse. But by mid-century it was taken over by an exiled Polish prince, Adam Czartorisky, who restored it with great taste and turned it into a haven for Polish patriots. Eugène Delacroix helped with the restoration of the LeBrun ceiling in the gallery. Now the house is one of the island's few privately owned residences. Most of the great houses facing the river as well as the smaller buildings on the interior streets have been converted to apartments like the one Suzanne and I rented on rue St-Louis-en-L'Ile.

During the 1920s, when Paris became a magnet for American expatriate literary figures such as Ernest Hemingway, Gertrude Stein, and Ford Maddox Ford, Ile St-Louis was their favorite meeting ground. Ford's *transatlantic review* and William Bird's Three Mountains Press both operated out of #29 Quai d'Anjou, and a restaurant on the ground floor of #33, Au Rendez-vous des Mariniers, drew crowds of expatriate writers. Today only an exceptionally successful writer or artist could afford to own an apartment on the island.

Our apartment was a two-floor walk-up with windows overlooking a drab central court. We tell ourselves that apartments are mostly for sleeping and views are an unnecessary luxury. This apartment consisted of a tiny kitchen, living room with dining table, bedroom and bath. After settling in we explored our neighborhood and did some basic grocery shopping. The high quality of the merchandise and the prices reflected the upscale character of the local trade. But on our first night we dined at Auberge de la Reine Blanche, a pleasantly unassuming establishment with friendly service, enjoyable fare, and modest prices. We also saved considerable sums by having two dinners at home. One of these evenings I was fighting off a slight cold; and taking it easy at home made for a quick recovery.

A general transportation strike this year caused us to do even more walking than usual. One walk took us to the Place des Vosges where we sat in the sun, read the *Herald Tribune*, watched young children at play in sand boxes, and developed appetites for a very enjoyable lunch at La Guirlande de Julie ('93 Michelin two forks, unlisted in '97 Michelin for no good reason in our judgment.) Specialties at this attractive mid-priced restaurant include chicken liver terrine, duck filet with mango sauce, and a delicious dessert of *fondant au chocolat*. On our recent stays in the Marais we have returned twice to enjoy the charm of this place. Its soothing pink and green decor evokes the era when Julie's garland was created, not of flowers but of thirty tender madrigals composed by her admirer.

On another walk we crossed the Pont de Sully to the Left Bank and sat on a bench in the outdoor sculpture garden on the Quai St-Bernard. This is one of the best vantage points for viewing the tip of Ile St-Louis and, further down river, the flying buttresses of Notre-Dame. In this park one sees a cross section of the Parisian public—fashionably dressed women leading fashionably groomed dogs, students from the nearby University of Paris bending over books or listening to tape players, and, of course, the ubiquitous Parisian lovers wrapped in blissful oblivion.

THE ROWING REGATTA

Nothing will ever match the spectacle I was lucky enough to catch one morning when I was out to stretch my legs along the Seine. I had seen an occasional oarsman in a single scull in years past, but I was bowled over when I caught the sight of six eight-oared shells racing up the river right next to Notre-Dame. They rounded the banks of La Cité, in an extremely difficult maneuver calling for great skill on the part of crew and cox and continued the race along the other side of the river. To my amazement this first group of shells was immediately followed by another heat of eights, then another and another. As a former oarsman at college and still a rowing enthusiast, I was absolutely transfixed by the colorful sight of these contending shells manned by crews in their club or college colors.

After the eights came an incredible diversity of other shells—four-man doubles and singles, pairs with and without coxswains, and single scullers. I gave up counting the numbers of contending boats, but there must have been over a hundred different entries. Men were predominant, but there were also quite a few women rowers, and some boats appeared to have mixed gender crews. Crowds lined the banks of the river and all the bridges, adding their cheers to the din of the coxswains' commands. The sight and sound still linger in my mind as one of the most exciting spectacles I've ever witnessed! I have now learned that the event, called the *Traversée de Paris* includes not only grueling twenty-five kilometer races but also, for those so inclined, leisurely rowing at your own pace.

BASILICA OF ST-DENIS

We took Metro Line 13 to see the ancient Abbey, now the Basilica of St-Denis, in the suburb of the same name about six miles north of Paris. The church is known principally as the first example of the Gothic style and as the burial site for many of the royal rulers of France. The Abbey was founded by Dagobert I on the spot where Saint Denis, the first Bishop of Lutetia, was interred. He retains a special place in the affection of Parisians for the rather remarkable feat associated with his martyrdom. Having been decapitated at around 250 A.D. in the area subsequently named Montmartre (hence the name), Saint Denis carried his gory head north to the site now bearing his name. On the way he reputedly stopped long enough to wash his head at a spot near the present Montmartre cemetery where a statue honors his memory.

Centuries after the remarkable exploits of Saint Denis his life came under the scrutiny of another monk, none other than Abélard, who had been exiled to the Abbey of St-Denis by superiors wanting to be rid of his troublesome antics. However, Abélard, living up to his reputation as an iconoclast, used his dialectic reasoning to prove that Saint Denis had been two different men. Since the abbey of St-Denis was a royal chapel, and this heretical finding was deemed an insult to the crown, Abélard was about to be hauled to trial before the King. But he escaped to the protective shield of the Count of Champagne in whose domain he lived for several years. Presumably monastic life at the Abbey resumed its placid pace after the departure of Abélard.

Pippin the Short and Charlemagne built the first three bays in the ancient basilica porch in the eighth century. The crypt, probably built over a Roman site, dates from the tenth or eleventh century. As the royal chapel and one of the richest churches of France, St-Denis became custodian of the Crown Jewels and royal ceremonial regalia which were subsequently transferred to the Louvre. During the first half of the twelfth century Abbot Suger, considered the originator of the Gothic style, presided over St-Denis. He began rebuilding the existing Romanesque structure in a revolutionary new design featuring pointed arches and large high windows that admitted penetrating light. This innovation and the enhancement of the windows by stained glass eventually became the preferred style for ecclesiastical building.

Almost a mirror of the history of the nation, St-Denis provides sanctuary for the tombs of the monarchs over a period of eight centuries. Among the exquisite carvings and effigies a notable collection is in the Bourbon vault in the crypt containing the remains of Louis XVI and Marie-Antoinette.

Another Bourbon, Louis XIV, was supposedly inspired to build Versailles because he so detested the view of St-Denis from the fortress/palace of Saint-Germain-en-Laye where he lived in semi-exile during his youth. Having to look at St-Denis is said to have reminded Louis that even the future Sun King was mortal. This seemingly petty annoyance, plus Louis's outrage when he found what his Supervisor of Finance had perpetrated in building Vaux-le-Vicomte, added impetus to his determination to build Versailles.

The last sovereign entombed at St-Denis is Louis XVIII, who authorized continuation of work started by Napoleon I to repair much of the damage done to the Abbey during the revolutionary sacking and pillaging in 1793. In 1837 the Northern tower was struck by lightning and had to be brought down. Eleven years later 1848 Viollet-le-Duc directed a thorough restoration leading to the structure we see today.

After touring the abbey we visited a very interesting archaeological museum next to the cloister. It displayed artifacts of early and on-going excavations as well as models of the abbey at various points in the past.

MUSÉE DES ARTS DECORATIFS

After a couple of abortive attempts in preceding years to visit this museum we finally gained admission on the last day of our 1993 Parisian sojourn. Earlier forays had been thwarted by changes in museum hours and closings of major sections for renovation. The museum occupies a wing of the Louvre facing the rue de Rivoli. This year friends had recommended that we see the Fabergé exhibition featuring pieces on loan from museums in Russia and elsewhere. Although jewel-encrusted eggs, crowns, miniature portraits, and other reminders of the opulence of the imperial court of the Tsars are certainly remarkable for their dazzling magnificence, they do not hold quite the same fascination for us as they do for many others. We spent relatively little time in this exhibition before moving on to the only other part of the museum then open to the public. It featured early twentieth century furniture and decorative objects we found interesting but not too appealing. The galleries that housed more interesting older French decorative art objects were again closed to the public. We left feeling a bit frustrated because, despite our several efforts, we had never seen the exhibits for which the museum is especially well known.

Next stop was the apartment for our final lunch to use up leftovers consisting of cold chicken, hard-boiled eggs, lettuce and tomato salad, Pont l'Eveque cheese, a baguette, Italia grapes, and, for me a delicious prune pastry. Not too bad a meal, considering!

Dinner with Ambassador Harriman's Speech Writer

For dinner we had arranged to meet Christopher Thompson, the son of our Washington neighbors, a tall, handsome young man with an engaging personality, a masterful command of the French language, a profound knowledge of French history, and an appreciation of French values and outlooks. Having lived much of his youth in Paris and Brussels where his parents were posted, he had become an enthusiastic fan of the great bicycle race, the Tour de France. Back in the United States for graduate study, he had chosen this famous sports spectacle as the subject of his doctoral dissertation when he was asked to become speech writer for then Ambassador Pamela Harriman.

We met him at Le 30, Fauchon, (three Michelin forks) the restaurant run by the famous food and wine purveyor, generally regarded as the premiere retail source of gourmet food and fine wines. Our dinner that night was memorable for the fare, the ambiance, and the conversation which centered on the challenges facing a speech writer in the Byzantine bureaucracy of the American embassy in Paris. Pulled out of academia, our young friend had had no prior experience in government, foreign affairs policy-making, or embassy politics. As his talents came to be recognized, he became a valuable staff asset not only as a writer but also as an advisor on French history, custom and style. Later, back in the States we were happy to hear that he had returned to academia and finished his dissertation on the history of the Tour de France entitled *"La Grande Bouclé,"* *A Social, Cultural, and Political History of the Tour de France Bicycle Race.* After some revision his thesis is to be published by the University of California Press.

My first course at Fauchon that evening was a delectable rabbit pâté, a house specialty. Suzanne has become very fond of rabbit dishes, and here is one of her current favorites.

RABBIT STEW IN WHITE WINE *serves 6 to 8*

1 rabbit weighing 4 to 5 pounds, deboned and cut
  into serving pieces
3 tablespoons bacon fat
2 tablespoons flour
2 cups chicken or beef stock
2 cups dry white wine
1 garlic clove, minced
1 bouquet garni
2 tablespoons tomato paste
2 tablespoons crème fraiche
salt and pepper

Heat fat in heavy casserole or skillet and brown rabbit pieces on all sides. Sprinkle with the flour, blend and add stock and wine. Add minced garlic, bouquet garni, tomato paste, salt and pepper.

Simmer, covered, over low heat for 1½ hours or until tender. Reduce sauce if necessary and stir in crème fraiche. Pour sauce over rabbit and serve.

Rue Des Grands Augustins, St-Germain-des-Prés

Wanting to try out a neighborhood in the sixth arrondissement which we had explored many times in the past, we selected an apartment at 25 rue Des Grands Augustins, three blocks in from the Seine in the sector known as St-Germain-des Prés. Our street led to the area known since medieval times as the Latin Quarter (since Latin was the common language of the academic residents), a lively and sometimes quite rowdy student quartier. It also features a busy and sometimes boisterous market district centering on rue de Seine and rue Buci. Market stalls line the sidewalks on these and several connecting streets creating a riot of color and aromas for the hordes of daily shoppers with the sing-song of the *chansoniers* or food hawkers filling the air.

After a little adjusting to the crowds and noise levels we came to feel at home in this exuberant atmosphere. We were each reminded of the youthful crowds that congregate in Washington, DC's Georgetown district on the weekends, but these revelers seemed good-natured and better behaved. (Incidentally, we always take earplugs with us to Paris—the only way of assuring a good night's sleep if the neighborhood proves to be noisy.)

We rented this studio apartment through a Chicago agency, Paris Séjour Reservations (PSR), selected from a French Government Tourist Office listing. This agency, which we used again in 1995, is one of over thirty listed in Appendix A. The apartment, tiny but recently renovated, was on the second floor of a building with no elevator. A group of old wooden beams had been erected vertically as room dividers between the sleeping and living areas. The French passion for exposed wooden beams (are they really old or simply distressed?) shows up in many apartment restorations. The French fondness for antiquity sometimes occurs at the expense of practical considerations such as closets, hooks for hanging clothes, full-length mirrors, efficient lighting, etc., but this apartment combined charm and a kitchen stocked with up-to-date utensils and tableware.

On our first day we explored the neighborhood while shopping in some of the countless food specialty shops and one of the two supermarkets. Just because we liked its looks (viewed from outside the back entrance it seemed a rather small, intimate place) we selected a restaurant for dinner, Le Procope (three red forks). By sheer chance we had stumbled on one of the most popular eating spots in Paris. On entering, we were surprised, first to find it a much bigger place than we had imagined, and second to realize that many of the hordes of diners were American tourists. Only afterwards on looking in the Michelin guide did we realize that we had happened on what is said to be the oldest café in Paris, founded in 1686 by an Italian who introduced coffee to the city. Early patrons included Voltaire, Rousseau, and Beaumarchais. In the nineteenth century the literati in attendance included George Sand, Victor Hugo, Guy de Maupassant, Emile Zola, and Balzac. Many of the choices on the menu are dishes which might well have been offered in that era. Sue chose a *blanquette* de veau while I sampled another house specialty, a lemony pasta dish in which a thin pasta combines with olive oil, black olives and thin strips of ham. This was a more up to date concoction than Le Procope's traditional specialties such as sausage-based *cassoulet*. Only back in our apartment did we read that we had been dining among the shades of some of France's most illustrious figures. Our dinner was the best possible introduction to our vibrant new neighborhood.

THE CHURCH OF ST-GERMAIN-DES-PRÉS

On our second day, we followed our usual pattern, taking things fairly easy to catch up with jet lag. In the morning we checked out more of the local shops noting the many traiteurs and promising food specialty places. While I took advantage of the bright sun for photographing and sketching, Suzanne enjoyed a short nap before we walked to the old abbey church that for centuries has lent its name to this part of Paris and to the well-known Boulevard St-Germain bisecting the area.

The origins of this church date to 542 AD when the son of Clovis, Childebert I, began constructing a holy place to house relics brought back from the Iberian peninsula. Frankish kings were buried here during the reigns of Pippin and Charlemagne. In 990 a new abbey was built over the early foundations, and it became the core of a small town then outside the walls of Paris. By the seventeenth century the abbey was one of Europe's leading intellectual centers, attracting scholars from far and wide.

The Revolution brought about the destruction of the abbey, the dispersal or execution of the monks and the burning of most of the fifty thousand books of the library. Only around a thousand were saved, which are now in the Bibliotheque Nationale.

All that remains of this ancient abbey complex are the present church and parts of the Abbot's palace, situated among ruins in a small but inviting close shaded by ancient trees. On the outside, only the tenth century clock tower porch with Moorish arches retains its original appearance. Inside an eleventh century Romanesque nave and choir are the oldest remnants of the original. During the nineteenth century restoration, a polychrome painting of wall murals and ceilings in royal shades of blue and red sought to emulate the original interior, an effect which came as a shock to Suzanne and me as we toured the interior. It was a far cry from the unadorned simplicity of the Cistercian and other monastic orders which we frankly prefer. Today St-Germain-des Prés and its churchyard, witnesses of an ecclesiastical presence on this site for some fifteen centuries, provide a welcome haven of tranquillity amid the busy hustle of Boulevard St-Germain.

In recent years this quarter has become one of the most fashionable residential areas of Paris and a gathering spot for discriminating and well-heeled shoppers, so much so that many observers are bemoaning the loss of the neighborhood's old character. What used to be a hangout for Parisian and expatriate intellectuals frequenting the many bookstores and cafes such as Café Flore and Deux Magots is now home to such upscale or trendy establishments as Louis Vuiton, Armani, Dior, Cartier, Benetton, and the Gap. Some locals take comfort in the fact that MacDonald's has yet to come on the scene.

Before this excursion we had spotted another restaurant just a block from the apartment, where, after checking in the Michelin, we had reserved a table for dinner. The Relais Louis XIII, (one star three forks) occupies a rustic half-timbered building that conjures a bygone era. The structure was actually built on the remains of the Grands

Augustins monastery and retains many of the amazingly preserved beams and paneling. On this site in May, 1610, the Dauphin was proclaimed King of France after the assassination of his father, Henri IV. We dined in a small cozy room furnished in period style. All went well until I sent the Maitre d' into a state of shock by ordering from the list of entrees a smoked salmon appetizer for my main course. What the French consider a normal three-or-four course dinner is much more than we can usually handle, and we invariably find ways to cut back. Suzanne and I often share dishes or order appetizers instead of main courses. Recently we find waiters more and more accepting of such bizarre behavior. Now even the doggy bag has gained at least partial acceptance, though we once had a hard time convincing a waiter that it would be all right to take home some of the mussels we could not finish. He was sure that we would be poisoned, but we persuaded him that, since the mussels had been cooked and would be in the fridge before we consumed them the next day, our request should be granted.

JARDIN DU LUXEMBOURG

Our apartment was close to one of the most beautiful and popular parks in Paris, the Jardin du Luxembourg. Nearly every year we manage to visit this welcoming space, where Parisians of all ages come to relax and enjoy the sun and greenery. The gardens are mostly formal though some areas follow the less formal English garden style. Other attractions include tennis courts, pony rides, playgrounds, and a large ornamental pool where children sail toy boats.

The grim and violent past of the Jardin is happily ignored by those enjoying its beauty and many amenities today. But in the post-Gallo-Roman era the area became a wilderness haunted by Vauvert, a ghostly highwayman whose lair consisted of an old ruin. In the thirteenth century the Carthusian monks persuaded Saint Louis to outlaw Vauvert and sanction the building of a huge monastery there.

Four centuries later Marie de Medici, the widow of Henri IV, decided to build a palace reminiscent of her native Tuscany, in particular, the Pitti Palace of Florence. While her new palace was being built, she commissioned a series of twenty-four enormous allegorical paintings by Rubens for the glorification of royalty and, incidentally, of her own life.

The Queen did not long enjoy her sumptuous new home. She had a falling out with the powerful Cardinal Richelieu, who persuaded her son, Louis XIII, to banish her to Cologne where she died penniless in 1642. Since Marie's time the Luxembourg Palace has been used for an extraordinary range of different purposes.

Louis XVIII, brother of Louis XVI, inherited the palace and lived here while plotting his return to the throne until his forced emigration in 1790. The palace was then converted into one of the more gruesome Parisian prisons, with bars at all the windows and cells whose walls bore the grim messages of prisoners about to be executed. Five years later, during the period of the Directory, the Luxembourg underwent another remarkable transition into residences of the five directors heading the executive branch of the new parliamentary government. Without fanfare Napoleon and the four other directors arrived in two hackney carriages to take apartments in a gutted and unfurnished shell. Later, when Napoleon assumed the rank of First Consul, he and Josephine lived at the Luxembourg in slightly less austere accomodations. Here Napoleon directed the monumental task of reorganizing the entire French political system.

In the nineteenth century the building was enlarged and the interior transformed into essentially its present physical state. During World War II the Germans occupied the building. After all these changes in the course of its history the palace has become the sedate seat of the French National Senate, or Upper House.

A wing of the palace houses a small museum in which we have enjoyed several shows of seasonal plants, flowers and, in particular, an exhibition of edible and poisonous mushrooms. Because of the French passion for mushrooms and the popularity of mushroom gathering in the wild, this display drew the largest number of viewers on the day of our visit.

In 1995 S. and I had the fun of meeting Sylvie for a picnic in the Luxembourg garden. The sun was bright enough to bring out dozens of sun-bathers eager to soak up the sun's autumnal rays before the onset of winter. A general strike that day had closed down nearly all public transportation, and all three of us came to the park on foot bringing a bottle of red wine, a baguette, cheeses, a duck liver pâté, grapes, and almond cookies we had purchased for the occasion. The idea of such an outing had probably never crossed the mind of our sophisticated friend, but she seemed delighted by the adventure. S. and I were sensibly dressed in jeans, walking shoes, and sport shirts, but Sylvie, the quintessential *soignée* Parisienne, wore a designer suit and lots of jangling gold bracelets. Her shoes did not look comfortable.

BRIE SANDWICH

Here is the recipe for one of our favorite picnic specials: Ingredients:

1 baguette sliced lengthwise
¼ cup olive oil,
2 cloves garlic, minced
10 oz. brie cheese, sliced
1 cup basil, shredded
3 tablespoons white wine
pepper to taste
3 teaspoons chives
1 ½ cups shredded sorrel leaves or other herb

Mix the garlic, herbs and oil. Sprinkle cut surfaces of baguette with oil and wine, thoroughly moistening the bread. Spread half of herbs and garlic on bottom half, and cheese slices on top half. Spread remaining herbs and garlic on brie. Put halves together, wrap in plastic, then in foil. Refrigerate with a weight on top for 4-5 hours or overnight. Serve along with *cornichons* or your other picnic favorites, sausages, or other cheeses.

CHÂTEAU DE CHANTILLY

This neo-Renaissance château is one of the several points of interest reachable by tourist buses such as those of Paris Vision. We signed up for a Sunday tour that lasted four and a half hours, including the thirty-five mile drive stretching beyond De Gaulle airport to the northeast. The château houses a fabulous collection of old-master and nineteenth-century paintings acquired by former owners of Chantilly, the Princes of Condé and the Duke of Aumale who bequeathed the estate to the Institute of France in 1886.

First owned as a hunting property by the Montmorency family in the fifteenth century, Chantilly has since undergone numerous additions and renovations. Surrounded by a small lake on three sides, the château and its beautiful gardens have much of the feeling of its contemporaries in the Loire Valley. Its famous art collection is housed in ten galleries overlooking the lake. Treasures include three Raphaels, works by Poussin, Ingres, Drouet, and Filippino Lippi as well as the *Book of Hours of Etienne Chevalier* with its 140 miniature paintings. The famed manuscript of *Les Très Riches Heures du Duc de Berry* is too delicate to be displayed. Because the Duke of Aumale stipulated in his

will that no paintings could be moved, they are displayed in the old tradition, crowding every inch of crimson damask wall space. One more modern gallery houses temporary exhibitions of contemporary works.

Chantilly is the site of one of the leading race courses and probably the grandest stables anywhere in the world. Built by the seventh Prince of Condé, who was convinced that he would be reincarnated as a horse, these stables would meet the needs of the most discriminating thoroughbred. They are now converted into the enormous Musée Vivant du Cheval, which holds daily dressage exhibitions. Today's visitor sees forty horses living in the luxury of the original stalls. During the summer months except August, when all of Paris is on vacation, the Hippodrome hosts races for two of France's most renowned trophies, the Prix Jockey-Club and the Prix de Diane-Hermès.

When thoroughbred horse racing first came to France from England around 1830 it brought an influx of English owners, trainers, grooms and stable boys. Before long an entire English community had moved across the channel to set up all the amenities that go with horse racing— inns, pubs, and bookmaking establishments. The owners built themselves English-style houses, schools, and churches of various denominations. This quasi-English settlement is peopled by descendants of the English immigrants—now French citizens with English names like Johnson, Brown or Jones. Similar communities exist in other cities such as Bordeaux and Pau where Englishmen settled generations ago and became totally integrated into their French surroundings.

In 1997, the centennial anniversary of the Duc d'Aumale's bequest of Chantilly to the Institut de France, many anniversary events were scheduled and a new catalogue of its collections was issued. An entire day should be devoted to visiting Chantilly, preferably a weekday when crowds are smaller. It is open daily except Tuesdays from March through October. The chateau is only thirty minutes by train from the Gare du Nord and is served by both RER and SNCF trains. The latter trains have more frequent departures, fewer stops en route, and more agreeable accommodations.

DINNER WITH THE AUTHOR OF *FRENCH OR FOE?*

Before leaving the states I had received a call from Polly Platt, an American who has lived in Paris for thirty years. Having published a timely and very readable book, *French or Foe?*, she was looking for advice on distributing her book in America. She felt that I could give her some tips based on experience with my book *Sojourn in Gascony*. Subsequently it has become abundantly clear from the huge success of her book that it was I who would learn from her. For our first meeting, Polly and her husband, Andé Grchich, invited us to dinner to trade ideas on book promotion.

The subtitle of her book explains what it's about, *"Getting the Most out of Visiting, Living and Working in France."* Polly's text explores the reasons why foreigners are so often provoked by French attitudes, why it is so hard to get information in France, why phone calls go unanswered, and generally why it takes so long to get business done. Polly draws on her own extensive experience, lacing her practical advice with a fine sense of humor and appreciation for the absurd predicaments that arise from lack of understanding.

S. and I agree with Polly's assessment that the French reputation for rudeness to foreigners, especially those who don't speak French, is too often overstated. The book cites many cases in which individuals have gone to great lengths in helping foreigners baffled by one or another problem. She offers one particular bit of advice we have followed with never-failing success. If you have a problem, whether seeking directions, finding some item in a shop, needing car repair or whatever, one should begin by saying *"Excusez-moi Monsieur (Madame) de vous déranger, mais j'ai un problème."* Invariably the person you approach will give you undivided attention and a polite and helpful response even if your French is somewhat shaky. The fact that you are trying works wonders.

Differences between the French and American national characters are so great and so deeply embedded in their respective psyches that they are not easily surmounted. But we share many common interests and a centuries-long history of helping each other in alliances against common enemies. In crass economic terms the fact is that American tourists and business executives living in France are vitally important to the French economy. In recent years France has undergone an enormous change in its attitude toward foreign investment. Today many American companies are joining firms of other nations in making direct investments in France, recently rated the least risky European economy except for Switzerland.

Americans have always had a love affair with French style and flair for living. *French or Foe?* shows how these shared interests at the national level can be buttressed by better interpersonal relationships. The book's enormous success (now going into its seventh reprinting with sales topping 70,000) is surely contributing significantly to better Franco-American relations.

Not too long after our dinner with Polly and Andé we had a chance to apply her advice when we were in our rented car in the town of Pau at the foot of the Pyrenees. We parked the car in an underground garage near the château we planned to visit. When it came time to move on from the garage, we discovered that you pay the fee by slipping the ticket into an automatic machine. It tells you how much you owe and, after you've paid, feeds you back a stub to open the barrier to the exit. Our only problem was that Suzanne, who had taken the ticket when we came in, now could not find it.

Following Polly's advice she approached an attendant and, in a self-deprecating way, recited the magic words (which translated mean "Excuse me for disturbing you, but I have this problem." He broke out in smiles and politely advised us that we could exit without our ticket at his booth. (Whether he would have been as accommodating if he'd heard the same words from me rather than my wife, we'll never know.) In fact, we did not have to take him up on this offer because we found the ticket on the floor of the car and exited legitimately.

The Crisis with the Telephone

Soon after our dinner conversation with Polly Platt touching on problems of daily life in Paris we faced what seemed at the time un *désastre* in our own apartment, demonstrating that apartment living, however much we enjoy it, is not entirely problem-free. For no apparent reason our antiquated rotary dial phone suddenly went dead, totally *en panne*, not even a dial tone. We were abruptly cut off from the outside world, and had to use a public phone in a nearby café, which had one on a wall in a cramped space adjacent to the WC. The jostling by a steady stream of customers and employees using the facilities reminded us that crowding in public places does little for people's manners.

Despite what used to be its poor reputation the French phone system is technically among the best in the world. Likewise, Parisian pay phones actually work very well, and we managed without much trouble to get through to our rental agency, which promised a repairman to replace our broken instrument the next day. The man appeared at the appointed hour, took out the broken telephone and replaced it with a new touchtone instrument. With a sigh of relief we resumed our phone-dependent life.

Nearly all the public phones in Paris now take micro-chipped cards *(télécartes)* as well as coins. You can use either personal credit cards or special phone cards which can be purchased in various amounts depending on your needs at post offices or *tabacs* (specially licensed newsstands or cafés). On recent visits we proudly completed several calls on our télécarte from pay phones. (As of October, 1996, every French telephone number was changed to a ten digit system. All Paris region numbers are preceded by 01. The zero is omitted only when calling from abroad.)

MONTMARTRE

Using our new phone, we called Sheila Hallsted, a young American woman and longtime resident of Paris who conducts private tours throughout the city. (See Appendix B for information on walking, jogging and biking tours and trails.) We signed Sheila up for a tour of her favorite places in Montmartre, called the Butte, or "mound" by Parisians. We knew that her itinerary would avoid the crowds and souvenir vendors around Sacré-Coeur. Years ago Sue and I separately had made the mandatory tourist visit to this landmark and neither of us was enamored of its Romanesque-Byzantine style, bright gilt, and gaudy iconography. However, one cannot fail to be impressed by the stunning impression of the church on the Paris skyline, especially at dusk and on a clear night. Construction of the church, which is dedicated to the cult of the Sacred Heart, began in 1877 and, was finished

forty-three years later. A place of pilgrimage for Catholics from all over the world, it is as much a Paris landmark as the Eiffel tower and enjoys two stars in the green Michelin.

In 1871, after Paris fell to the Prussians, thousands of local citizens were slaughtered in a hopeless defense of this hilltop. They are buried in the cemetery on the eastern side of the hill and were commemorated by the building of the Sacré Coeur Basilica. Martyrs have been meeting their death here since at least the third century AD. Among the first was Saint Denis who, as we noted earlier, carried his own head from here to the area north of Paris which now bears his name.

Another big tourist attraction included in our walk was the world-famous Bohemian gathering place, the Place du Tertre. In this lively square local artists display their work, most of which is intended as tourist souvenirs of Paris. Though their work may fall more in the realm of "kitsch" than "great art," discriminating viewers can find real talents represented, and the square is well worth a visit if only for its lively atmosphere.

We lingered a good while in the ancient church of St-Pierre, one of the oldest in Paris. Dating to the twelfth century, it is the only remaining structure of the Abbey of Montmartre founded by Queen Adélaide of Savoy, wife of Louis VI, known as "the Big." Inside are four marble columns crowned with capitals attributed to a Roman temple that once stood atop the mountain. Subsequent restorations have largely succeeded in maintaining the purity and simplicity of the original structure.

We walked from the church along old crooked streets, past the Clos Montmartre, the vineyard where on the first Saturday of October the start of the French grape harvest is celebrated. The wine which, as noted earlier is improving, can be purchased at the Mairie (Mayor's Office) of Montmartre. Our tour then took us to an old tavern now called the Lapin Agile. Early Bohemian artists and writers began a tradition of literary evenings that continues to this day. Cabaret acts are occasionally presented on a small stage. Simple tavern fare is provided. The tavern's present name is a pun based on the early nineteenth century sign painted for it, a rabbit escaping the cook's pot, by André Gill. Another well-known landmark we passed on our walk was the Moulin de la Galette, the oft-painted windmill that has topped the hill for more than six centuries. Both the windmill and the eponymous turn of the century dance hall inspired such painters as Renoir and Van Gogh.

Adjacent to the vineyard is the rambling Museum of Old Montmartre holding mementos of Bohemian life and the renowned figures who lived and worked in the area, including Bernard, Renoir, Utrillo, Dufy, and the composer Charpentier. In addition to permanent exhibitions of the great Impressionists the museum presents temporary exhibitions of work by current artists. We had time only for a cursory tour of this enchanting museum and the lovely garden behind it.

We paused for lunch in the rear garden of Le Moulin de la Galette da Graziano, an Italian restaurant where we sat in a charming garden under an ancient chestnut tree. Delicious antipasti and a veal scallopini accompanied by a Chianti table wine provided a diversion from French cuisine while also girding us for the second part of our tour. Sheila then led us to some of Montmartre's quiet residential streets lined with grand ivy-covered houses, handsome trees and groomed shrubbery. The most enchanting part of this walk took us through a strictly private passageway whose gate happened to be unlocked because of some utility work under way. Sheila boldly led us into the Hameau des Artistes, a succession of intriguing back yards and small gardens. Some were really kitchen gardens with small vegetable patches and an occasional fruit tree; some had children's swings and play houses; others featured sculpture placed in more formal settings.

Montmartre's eclectic architectural styles reflect the changing periods and tastes of those who lived and labored here and, in the process, created a universally appealing atmosphere.

THE RICHELIEU WING OF THE LOUVRE

As a bonus, our apartment rental agency in Chicago had provided passes for an evening tour of the newly opened Richelieu wing of the Louvre. The Richelieu wing is yet another of I. M. Pei's fantastic architectural achievements, which must be experienced first hand to be fully appreciated. Aside from the many masterworks housed within it, the breathtaking scale of the space, its magnificent Second Empire (1852 - 71) staircase and the sweeping views from its upper windows are incentive enough for an extended visit.

Four floors of galleries compose the Richelieu wing. The collections range from Islamic and Oriental to French sculpture and painting and artworks of the Northern School—notably Flemish, Dutch and German. Our tour concentrated mainly on the French and Northern School galleries, and even so we seemed to be skimming the surface. One immense gallery on the second floor displays the twenty-four large Rubens canvases based on the life of Marie de Medici, second wife of Henri IV. It seems ironic that she should be remembered in the wing of the Louvre named for the Cardinal responsible for her fall from power. Could this be Marie's posthumous revenge?

One of the few examples of Second Empire interiors to have survived along with many of its original furnishings is on view in the apartments of Napoleon III and Eugénie, open to the public since 1993. He oversaw vast renovation of the Louvre including the grandiose facades on the Seine. The rich, some might say garish, display of gold, crystal, crimson damask and velvet in these apartments is the ultimate in lavish ornamentation, and the chandeliers lit at night are a spectacular sight. Everything glitters in unrestrained abandon. But for some viewers, including us, the gaudy excess of this style marks a low point in the evolution of French decor.

Designed for Napoleon III in 1861, the apartments were appropriated by the Ministry of Finance ten years later, with the fall of the Second Empire, and have remained as the intermittent offices of the Ministry and the opulent setting for its official receptions. But while the renovation of the Louvre wing was under way the Ministry moved its offices to a temporary site on the Left Bank. Then a major furor arose when Edouard Balladur became Finance Minister and, despite his effort to portray himself as an advocate of budgetary restraint and government downsizing, decided to move the Ministry offices back into these apartments. Greatly enamored of their ornate splendor, he added to it by requisitioning antiques from the Louvre storerooms while ordering new livery for his white-gloved footmen. He held on to these quarters until the Socialists came to power in 1988 and the new Finance Minister vacated the premises for a less prestigious address.

• • •

Napoleon III and Baron Haussmann

Although Emperor Napoleon III (who started out as Louis Napoleon) and his famous protegé, Baron Haussmann, have been mentioned several times, I have not given enough attention to the lasting legacy of their planning and building in Paris. Historians generally estimate that sixty percent of present-day Paris was actually built during the eighteen creative years of the Second Empire, thus the story of the two figures who were responsible deserves a closer look.

Napoleon's main claim to the French throne rested on a flimsy assertion that he was the nephew of Napoleon Bonaparte, though most people suspected he was the product of one of his mother's less exalted liaisons. His convictions about his descent and his extraordinary ambition led him to try anything to attain the throne. Following two failed coups launched against the Orleanist regime of Louis Philippe, Louis Napoleon managed to win election as president of the Second Republic in 1848. Only four years later he engineered a popular referendum that won nearly universal support for an end to the republic and a return to empire. Thus began an amazing era, sometimes called the Age d'Or, in which Paris was propelled from urban decrepitude into modernity.

Napoleon had grandiose ideas and the courage to pursue them. He bestowed on Haussmann the title of Baron, named him prefect of the Seine, and gave him almost dictatorial powers to tear down and rebuild the city. Under their joint direction Paris acquired a technologically advanced sewer system (still a major tourist attraction), a network of straight wide boulevards, a series of elegant squares, and the handsome, austere architectural style of nearly all residential housing so characteristic of Paris. They set limits on building heights and imposed a uniformity of style for the facades. Strict style standards were also imposed on public amenities—fountains, street lamps, and sidewalks. Of course, to build Haussmann's boulevards planners had to tear down untold thousands of houses, displacing the unfortunate occupants. But the results of the planning and rebuilding were so spectacular that opposition had little chance of prevailing. Paris became a mecca for foreign travelers, whose fat wallets assuaged many citizens' doubts.

The most famous landmark erected during this period is the Paris Opera, now usually called the Opéra Garnier in honor of its architect, Charles Garnier. Now the third most-visited tourist site in Paris after the Eiffel Tower and the Arc de Triomphe, this building is an overwhelming display of unrestrained embellishment and all-out commitment to grandeur both inside and out. A hodge-podge of architectural styles, it nevertheless makes a strong statement and is now accepted as an essential part of the city. After a costly renovation Opéra Garnier reopened in the spring of 1996 to become an alternative site to the much criticized ultra modern Opéra Bastille discussed below. Both opera houses are managed today by a central administration that selects programs and sets schedules for each venue. Although Opera Bastille productions usually play to full houses, one has to wonder if Baron Haussmann is spinning in his grave over the intrusion of such an architectural monstrosity.

Napoleon's empress, Eugénie, also exercised a tremendous influence on French style and culture. Though she, like her husband, was ridiculed as a *parvenu* (she was born to a family of Spanish lesser nobility), she had the power to dictate taste. Blessed with a lovely complexion and a remarkable bosom, her choice of wardrobe sent necklines plunging. Hoop skirts became *de rigeur*, bringing about an entire industry to furnish the iron for the hoops. She shocked the gentry by daring to ride astride rather than sidesaddle.

When the imperial court made its regular seasonal move to Napoleon's preferred palace at Compiègne, the glitterati of Paris were invited to spend a week in the country. Court etiquette dictated that ladies must change their attire three times a day, and that each dress should be worn only once. Socially ambitious Parisians hardly dared to decline invitations to Compiègne, but some went broke for the sake of making a fashionable appearance. The old Parisian aristocracy, however, held the emperor and his followers in contempt as *nouveaux riches* totally lacking in taste and refinement. Although Napoleon III has retained a place in history for his accomplishments in city planning and other good works, it remains a fact that the court's excesses and widespread corruption greatly contributed to the downfall of the Second Empire.

THE CHAMPS ELYSÉES

The most famous boulevard in Paris, the Champs Elysées, though it was laid out well before Haussmann's time, was a crucial element in all of his planning. Now part of what is called the Grand Axis stretching from the Arc du Carrousel in the Louvre to the Arc de Triomphe in Place Charles de Gaulle and on beyond to the Arche of La Défense, the Champs Elysées is the avenue most familiar to the majority of

American, British, and other tourists. The first leg of this route from the Tuileries to the Rond Point des Champs Elysées was begun under direction of Louis XIV's master landscaper, Le Nôtre, in 1664. Napoleon decided to build the Arc De Triomphe in 1806. La Défense was one of the monumental architectural legacies of President Francois Mitterand.

Ever since huge crowds gathered to greet Napoleon I on returning from his victories the Champs Elysées has been a focal point of French national pride. General de Gaulle marched in triumph along this route after the Liberation. Monumental in design and function, the great avenue has come to represent the city's grandeur and prestige.

Americans visiting Paris for the first time may feel more at home on the Champs Elysées than in other quarters because of the movie theaters featuring American films, the shops catering to American tastes, the restaurants with English language menus, and Le Drugstore, the original establishment signaling the Americanization of French culture. Older generations of Parisians trying to resist this American intrusion seem to have been overwhelmed by younger generations ready and eager to emulate their American counterparts. No place in Paris better exemplifies the process of cross-culturalization than this famous thoroughfare. But visitors should recognize that the Champs is no more typical of Paris than, for example, 42nd Street is typical of New York City or Piccadilly typical of London.

VERSAILLES, THE ROYAL VEGETABLE GARDEN

Our final excursion before leaving Paris this year was a visit to Versailles, *not* to the chateau but to the Potager du Roi, the great fruit and vegetable garden established by Louis XIV to feed the three thousand people who populated his court. The word *potager* stems from the word for soup, later applied to the chef who made the soup and finally to the garden in which the ingredients were grown. This magnificent complex, remarkably, has survived the last three centuries virtually intact.

We took the RER Line C-5 to Versailles (about a half-hour ride). Our first stop, as always when we visit Versailles, was the bike rental shop, a short walk down to the right of the fountains and gardens of the central axis. We always bypass the interior of the palace, which is swarming with visitors, and cycle for miles along the wonderful gravel walkways. In addition to the potager, we were keen to see the recently restored Hameau de la Reine, the farm hamlet built so that Marie-Antoinette could indulge her fantasy of living a simple peasant life. The hamlet, complete with barnyard goats, sheep, geese, and ducks, surrounds a lovely lake and offers a charming diversion from the formality of the chateau and Le Nôtre's gardens. After returning our bikes we went in search of a restaurant aptly named the *Potager du Roy*. There we enjoyed a fine lunch featuring a ragout of veal with assorted vegetables and a caramelized fig dessert, such as might have delighted the *Roi Soleil* himself.

We reached the entrance to the potager just in time to catch a guided tour led by a horticulturist staff member. We learned that the Sun King had a passion for vegetables and fruits and that he took tremendous pride in the diversity of produce and the ability to grow his favorites almost throughout the year. Among these were asparagus, cauliflower, radishes, lettuces, and figs. Fermenting manure packed around the plants assured a supply of the King's special favorites through long growing periods. Figs were produced over a six month period from early Spring to late Fall. State visitors to Versailles were almost always given a personal tour of the garden by the King. From a parapet he could survey the yearly cycle of planting, tilling, grafting, pruning, and harvesting. Tunnels under the parapet made excellent root cellars. The designer of this garden, Jean de la Quintinie, used a variety of hotbeds, cold frames and cloches to create different microclimates for the growing of out-of-season produce.

Our tour took us through the checkerboard of tidy squares or garden "rooms," decorative as well as practical, each with its special planting. Low-growing and artfully pruned fruit trees and vineyards flourish in spaces shielded against wind and cold by stone walls. Elaborate irrigation systems convey water to all parts of the complex. Even for one as uninformed as I about gardening, the visit was tremendously rewarding, and Suzanne, the garden enthusiast was fascinated. Here is a recipe for a soup made from one of her favorite vegetables grown not only in the potager but also in our Washington garden.

SORREL SOUP *Serves 8-10 Serve hot or cold*

2 cups sorrel leaves, washed and stems removed
1 medium size onion, sliced
4 small (or 3 medium) boiling potatoes, peeled and
 chopped
juice of ½ lemon
½ cup cream (optional) or milk
salt and pepper to taste

Heat stock in saucepan. Add sliced onion and sorrel leaves. Simmer until sorrel leaves are wilted. Add potatoes and cook 45 minutes or until potatoes are tender. Purée in blender or force through food mill. Add salt and pepper, lemon juice and cream.

Ile St-Louis, Second Rental

$\mathcal{I}$n 1995 we arranged six months in advance to return to our favorite part of Paris, thus taking advantage of the discounts offered by the rental agency (again PSR in Chicago) and by the airline for early booking. As time passed, we became somewhat apprehensive about the series of bombings by Algerian terrorists in Paris and other major French cities. We kept abreast of these activities through the U.S. media, and also by listening to French language news programs, which I often do while shaving, and through contacts with the French Embassy. News was not exactly reassuring——bombs were planted in trash cans and under subway car seats wherever they might inflict the greatest damage. A bomb had taken a heavy toll at St-Michel Metro station, one of the busiest in Paris, near where we planned to stay.

Weighing all the risks, and recognizing that the death toll in our home town routinely exceeds that of the terrorist bombs in Paris, we decided to proceed with our plans, but cautiously. We would avoid rush hours in the busy Metro stops, use buses whenever feasible, and walk as much as possible. Once in Paris we found that people were for the most part taking the situation in stride. The most notable change was the sealing of trash cans. This, of course, created problems for the trash collectors and street cleaners as well as pedestrians and Metro riders. Security was greatly stepped up wherever we went, and some of the terrorists were caught. During our week in Paris another bomb exploded near the southern perimeter of the city and, after we had left, the most devastating of the bombs was set off in a subway train between stations not far from our apartment. Aside from curtailing our use of the subway a bit, the bombings had little effect on us: we adopted the Parisians' resigned attitude. Sometimes it seems that the typical Parisian simply pretends that there is no crisis.

OUR APARTMENT

The location of this apartment on rue Des Deux Ponts, one of the two main streets crossing Ile St-Louis, was convenient but more exposed to heavy traffic than we would have wished. Noise was not a real problem however, since we had our ear plugs and only one of our windows opened on the street. Compared with other apartments we have rented this one was short on charm, but otherwise entirely livable.

The real plus for this location was its proximity to shopping, restaurants, post office, and the bookstore that carries the *Herald Tribune*. I could choose from three bakeries all on rue St-Louis en L'Ile for croissants, baguettes, and other breads on my pre-breakfast outing to pick up the *Tribune*. We felt at home in the familiar surroundings of St-Louis, the shop windows with all their weird and wonderful gizmos and the galleries exhibiting local artists. Prices as always ranged from high to out of sight, and there has been a fair amount of turnover among the shops. The Salon de Thé turned into a poetry shop, as noted earlier, was one example of such change.

On the western tip of the island are two cafés with sizable outdoor terraces looking out across the Seine to Notre-Dame. S. and I often pause in whichever of these cafés has the best table available for people-watching. Happily, it's impossible to go very far in Paris without finding such places.

PALAIS-ROYAL

The objective of our first excursion this year was the Palais-Royal, the imposing palace facing the square in front of the Louvre that now houses the Council of State. Neither of us had visited this prominent landmark in the center of Paris or knew of its many important roles in the city's history. Such ignorance demonstrated once more how much there is to learn about Paris and how, despite our many visits, we are still skimming the surface.

In 1632 Cardinal Richelieu commissioned the building of the initial section as his residence. Later expansion resulted in the enormous edifice now standing. Nothing illustrates the Cardinal's power more clearly than the strategic location of the palace and its gardens. Two wings extending behind at great length behind the front section face each other across a huge garden space. The Cardinal and his retinue occupied the palace until his death, in 1642, when he left it to Louis XIII, who soon followed Richelieu to his grave. The king's widow, Anne of Austria, with her son, Louis XIV, then quit the Louvre for this palace which was renamed the Palais-Royal. But the Fronde, the popular uprising against the onerous taxation imposed by Richelieu's successor, Cardinal Mazarin, forced the young king and his mother to abandon the Palais-Royal for Saint-Germain-en-Laye. Later, when Louis XIV returned to Paris, he chose to move into the Louvre instead of the Palais-Royal. In 1649, his cousin, King Charles of England, was beheaded and Louis, an ardent believer in the divine right of kings, offered the Palais-Royal as a residence for Charles' widow, Henrietta.

Over the years the palace housed a succession of royals including Louis-Philippe of Orléans who, needing to supplement his income, initiated the construction of the apartment houses with ground level shopping arcades surrounding the garden. A stroll through these arcades today conveys a sense of how the palace precinct became a fashionable meeting place not only for the well-heeled *haut monde* who congregated there but also for the *demi-monde* and people from all ranks of society. In the pre-revolutionary era it harbored pamphleteers and demagogues railing against the monarchy and the aristocracy.

It was more placid and less crowded on our stroll under the arcade. Several restaurants were setting up outdoor tables as we walked along. The shop windows displayed articles appealing to collectors: miniature soldiers representing all eras of French military history, old medals and decorations for distinguished service, stamps, and even the couture of famous twentieth-century Parisian designers. As we were admiring the planting in the garden, we heard the great boom of the Palais-Royal toy cannon, which goes off at midday whenever the sun, reflected through a magnifying glass, is strong enough to ignite the charge.

SHAKESPEARE & CO.

Among English-speaking residents of Paris, especially intellectuals and foreign students, no place equals the venerable bookstore, Shakespeare & Co., as a gathering place, information exchange center, and source of cultural nourishment. On the left bank, opposite Notre-

Dame, this establishment is the successor to the first English-language lending library in Paris, founded by Sylvia Beach in 1919. From the start it drew into its circle most of the English-speaking literati who lived and worked near or on Ile St-Louis. James Joyce, Ezra Pound, Ernest Hemingway,  Thornton Wilder, Scott Fitzgerald, Sherwood Anderson, and Gertrude Stein made Shakespeare & Co. their hangout. Walt Whitman was a special favorite of the founder, who began the tradition of an annual Whitman reading on the first Monday in February.

While it calls itself a store for antiquarian books, it houses an eclectic collection of mostly English-language titles in a haphazard non-system of floor-to-ceiling shelves and piles on piles of books. Every conceivable field or period seems to be represented, but the emphasis remains on the golden age of the post-1918 American invasion of Paris. Browsing is encouraged, and if a reader should want to buy, the proprietor, George Whitman, a grandson of Walt Whitman, or one of his assistants handles the transaction at the cluttered front desk. A computerized tracking system like those in most modern bookstores would seem the very last thing Shakespeare & Co. would ever contemplate. The amazing memories of Whitman and his assistants permit them to locate titles and keep account of stock. But commerce in books seems almost an incidental mission for this establishment, which has always been a kind of home for itinerant writers and an information exchange center. Above the bookstore are three rooms with beds which Whitman offers to serious writers for a week's stay at no charge.

A motto inscribed over a doorway summarizes the guiding philosophy: "Be not inhospitable to strangers lest they be angels in disguise." In keeping with this principle, those in need of overnight shelter may be able to bed down in one of the tiny book-lined rooms upstairs. Outside are benches for the browsers and, on the weathered storefront, a blackboard for personal notices. In addition to searches for housing, jobs, addresses, and phone numbers of missing relatives and friends, there are such touching advertisements as one we noted, "Modest expatriate wishes to correspond with girl who has a tragic sense of life and a magical sensitivity to people."

Not long after my book, *Sojourn in Gascony*, was published and I was taking it to Parisian bookstores I showed it to George Whitman. He made a cursory examination of the book and, in a gesture typical of his generous spirit, offered to take some copies on consignment. As he filled out a receipt form for the transaction, it was evident that his main motive was giving at least a small break to a novice writer. He told me to come back and collect the proceeds from the sales on my visit to Paris the following year.

When I did show up the next year with receipt in hand, he seemed a bit baffled, obviously not recalling a small transaction a year ago. He could not possibly have remembered whatever became of my little paperbacks thrown in with his vast inventory, but without hesitation he reached into his pocket and produced the franc notes to pay for my books.

THE GENERAL STRIKE

Much of Paris closed down during a one-day strike of *fonctionnaires*—government employees, especially transport workers, teachers, and museum employees. That was the day that we met Sylvie in the Jardin de Luxembourg for a picnic lunch and managed easily without public transportation. The strike was a precursor of those to come later in the year to protest le Plan Juppé, the then Prime Minister's multipronged austerity program. These widespread actions disrupted daily life in Paris even more than the terrorist bombings.

Whether measured in terms of numbers of marchers, lost days of work, business bankruptcies, or the impact on the national economy, the strikes indicated the intensity and breadth of disaffection with government policy. As the 1997 elections proved so convincingly, the efforts of the Juppé administration to reduce public spending and qualify for the Euro currency initiative won few converts and alienated many. France is by no means the only West European nation to confront this dilemma, but you would never know it from the public debate in France.

The one-day strike had very little effect on S. and me. We walked to our picnic in the Luxembourg, something we probably would have done in any case. The walk also gave us the chance to search out the site of one of Leslie Clevenger's photos from which I had painted the statue of the honorable cleric with the pigeons. Leslie had not been sure where the photo had been taken, but before we left for Paris she told me that it was near the church of Saint Sulpice. We found it, still serving as a roost for the pigeons, at the top of a huge fountain in front of the church. We also determined that the subject, François de Salignac de la Mothe Fénelon, (1651-1715) Archbishop of Cambrai, was one of the most influential and controversial clerics of his era. He served as tutor in the court of Louis XIV until being banished to his bishopric when his book, *Télémanque*, was condemned by Pope Innocent XII.

Another serendipitous discovery made on this walk was the site of Leslie's photo of the hat shop. By merest chance I spotted this shop on rue St. Sulpice. It looks very much as it did when the photo was taken a few years ago. Different hat styles, but still eye-catching. Only recently have I learned that Agnès b is a world famous designer with 110 boutiques scattered around the globe. Her incredible career began in 1979 when her simple pearl-snap cardigan appeared. Now her twice-yearly collections of casual classic clothes for men, women, and children are highlights of the fashion world. Prices are affordable and, best of all, designs are not keyed to the fashion of the moment but for keeps.

Yet another painting depicts Leslie Clevenger taking a photo of a Metro entrance, this one at Abbesses in the north of Paris. Eighty-four of the street entrances to the

Metro system used to be distinguished by these wrought-iron wonders designed by Hector Guimard at the turn of the last century. Now, in the search for a more modern look, these gracious reminders of an earlier era are being torn down, to the great dismay of many Parisians and foreigners as well. This face lift of Metro stations costing $60 million was completed in 1996. Nostalgia buffs regret the removal of these old stations not only because of their elegance but also as useful visual markers of subway entrances.

For our dinner engagement the night of the general strike, we had to take quite a long walk, this time to our favorite restaurant, Le Petit Laurent, where we met Polly Platt and husband, Andé, who had biked from their apartment. A delicious lobster bisque introduced a meal that lived up to all expectations. Other dishes we selected were a curried scallop casserole with mushrooms, and a *blanquette* of pork with ginger, two of the more recent additions to the menu. We have become such regulars in this establishment that we are always greeted warmly by the maitre d' and seated at what has become "our" table.

Biking, Jogging, and Walking

Polly and Andé are among the many stalwart Parisian bicyclists who realize that this form of transportation offers many advantages in a city notorious for its horrendous traffic problems. The city government encourages bicycling as a pollution-free approach to traffic circulation. Bikers find quite a few places where they can ride in the larger parks such as Bois de Boulogne and Bois de Vincennes while other bike tracks have been constructed along routes noted in Appendix B which also provides a source for bike rentals. Amazingly enough, most Paris drivers are quite patient and courteous with bicyclists. Also in Appendix B is information on paths for walkers and joggers. A little known footpath, *grande randonée*, links the ten miles between the Bois de Boulogne and the Bois de Vincennes. It takes about three hours to walk the distance. The Office of Tourism also provides lists of groups conducting walking tours of various sections of the city.

No discussion of Paris walkways should fail to mention the most popular bridge over the Seine leading from the Institut de France to the Louvre, namely the Pont des Arts. Built in 1803 as a toll bridge for pedestrians, it was rebuilt later and opened to the public without tolls. In good weather this bridge boasts an assortment of musicians, mimes and artists taking advantage of the spectacular views of the river and its banks. I find it an ideal spot for quick sketching.

SAINT-GERMAIN-EN-LAYE

One beautiful sunny morning (the weather this October was unusually fine) we set off for Saint-Germain-en-Laye via a short Metro ride and a twenty-two minute trip on the RER (line A-1). The palace at Saint-Germain dates to the early twelfth century when the Capetian kings built a feudal fortress on massive foundations that appear today just as one ascends the escalator from the RER. They serve as the base of the chateau built in Renaissance style by Francis I, who found this site and its great hunting preserves much to his liking.

Saint-Germain is more closely identified with a long line of French monarchs than any palace outside of Paris. Its situation on top of an escarpment looking out on the city and the vast park surrounding it explain its centuries-long appeal. While many French rulers left their mark on the building and grounds, Louis XIV had by far the greatest impact. He was born here, and lived here for most of his first twenty years.

The small room in which Louis was born is in a building now called the Pavillon Henri IV, a restaurant and hotel adjacent to the main palace. In accordance with royal protocol, ranking courtiers were summoned as witnesses to the birth of an heir to the throne. Scores of princesses, duchesses, and court officers crowded into this little room to watch as Anne of Austria delivered Louis, her first-born child. The fact that Anne had taken twenty-two years to conceive, coupled with the widespread belief that Louis XIII was considered incapable of siring any offspring, made this birth a particularly momentous occasion. A six-day national celebration ensued with Te Deums in the churches, free wine flowing from an obelisk outside the birth site, canons firing royal salutes, and dancing in the streets. While the French citizenry joined in the festivities, court plotters and scandal-mongers charged that the true father of Louis was Anne's powerful mentor and favorite, Cardinal Mazarin.

Growing up in a kind of exile at Saint-Germain, Louis became increasingly disenchanted with Paris, whose skyline dominated the view from the palace grounds. The landscaping of these grounds had been carried out under a succession of leading designers, and culminated in the work of the most illustrious of them all, Le Nôtre, who oversaw extensive remodeling between 1662 and 1674. When Louis decided to build Versailles, he turned again to Le Nôtre to draw up the more grandiose landscape plan for the new royal seat. More recently the gardens and terraces at Saint-Germain have benefited from a major restoration after some years of relative neglect, and they now rival the palace as an attraction for tourists. Outdoor snack bars provide simple fare for those preferring to eat *en plein air*.

An excellent archaeological museum occupies large parts of two main floors of the palace; exhibitions range from prehistoric to Gallo-Roman times. Most of the artifacts come from various parts of France, but acquisitions from locations all around the world allow comparisons among different civilizations. The collection we found most interesting consists of plaster maquettes of Roman buildings, including the fora in Nimes, Arles, and Orange, the Maison Carrée, and the Pont du Gard. The chapel was the only interior area of the palace we saw still in its original state.

After our tour we walked across the square to a restaurant with a good view of the palace, the Brasserie du Théatre. The dashing waiter who served us sported a flamboyant reddish handle-bar mustache. We debated whether it would annoy him if I asked to take his picture, but, when I did, we realized that this was a common occurrence. He posed readily, while one of his fellow waiters teased him for being so eager to show off his mustache. Suzanne praised the crème brulée as the best she had tried during this week in Paris.

MUSÉE CARNAVALET

This museum, like the Palais-Royal, is a place we should have visited before in order to learn about the history of Paris. Its collections, housed in two separate mansions linked by a first floor gallery, focus on the history of the city. The Hôtel Carnavalet, from which the museum derives its name, covers the period up to 1789, and the smaller Hôtel Le-Peletier-St-Fargeau continues from the Revolution to the present. Both houses are historically and architecturally significant. The

Marquise de Sevigné, whose letters vividly described events in the years 1677 to 1696, lived in the Hôtel Carnavalet.

On the ground floor an exhibit of the origins of the city up to the end of the Middle ages includes fascinating models, maps, charts, and ancient artifacts showing how Paris evolved. Another four rooms on this floor present the history of Paris during the Renaissance and the Wars of Religion. On the second floor are rooms devoted to the life of Mme. de Sevigné and Paris during the Ancien Régime. The Hôtel Le Peletier with its paintings and objets d'art dating from the Revolution has one room containing the furniture of the royal family during their confinement in the Temple. The museum has been decorated throughout with beautiful paneling and murals from other great Paris houses. A huge Brunetti painting, originally in a house on Boulevard Saint-Germain, adorns the imposing staircase leading to the first floor.

We have visited the Carnavalet in two consecutive years and still feel we have not given it as much time as it deserves. For those wishing to get to know Paris we can think of no better place to start. Added attractions are a first-rate gift shop and library.

For our last evening in Paris on this visit we reserved a table at L'Orangerie, a restaurant just a few paces from our apartment. We had dined there on one of our earlier stays. A rave review in *Le Figaro* led us to try it again, and we were thrilled that we did.

L'Orangerie's loyal clientele and refined ambiance evoke an era not too long ago when diners dressed elegantly, jewels glowed in the flickering light of table candles and wall sconces, and gentleness prevailed. This thirty-some year old establishment is a far cry from many newer restaurants catering to younger generations who prefer to dress casually and to dine in a less subdued atmosphere. In recent years the restaurant has been discovered by the Parisian glitterati who appreciate its atmosphere of refinement. Only a small brass plaque and a pair of elegantly clipped shrubs in sidewalk planters identify L'Orangerie from outside. In keeping with this low profile the owner prefers not to be listed in either the Michelin, Gault Millau or Hachette guides. Regardless, the habitués keep coming back, and reservations must be made well in advance. Only dinner and late supper are served.

The menu is so limited that it fits on one small page. Most regular customers depend mainly on their waiter to recite the evening's choices and proffer recommendations. Restaurant tradition stressing congenial and attentive service extends both to regular and first-time clientele, and a complimentary bottle of a fine Bordeaux, (a Chateau de Barre when we were there) and mineral water are provided. After this delightful final evening we added L'Orangerie to our list of preferred restaurants.

Usually we celebrate our last evening in Paris by dining at a favorite restaurant. But if we want an evening at home before an early departure Suzanne likes to do something with what scraps may be left in the fridge.

Gratin des Restes (Gratin of Leftovers)

It is not possible to list ingredients by quantities because all depends on what leftovers you have. But as bistro chefs know, a delicious and imaginative gratin can be composed of whatever you have such as meat, poultry, fish, vegetables, cheese, or eggs. You may cook the vegetables lightly or not at all as you prefer. (Carrots, for instance, should be cooked first). Mix solid ingredients together with a minced garlic clove and some chopped onion, both sautéed, in a bowl. Bind them with a creamy bechamel sauce with grated cheddar or gruyere cheese. An alternative is a sauce made from a condensed soup such as tomato slightly thinned with sour cream or yogurt and well seasoned. Mix sauce into ingredients in bowl and transfer to a buttered shallow baking dish, sprinkle cheese on top and bake in 350°F oven fifteen minutes until top is golden and bubbling. Such a gratin along with a salad and wine consumed in the privacy of your apartment can be a memorable (and economical) way to mark your final evening in Paris.

Fontainebleau

After this week in Paris we drove down through Burgundy as far as the Dordogne. We decided to make the first day's drive an easy one—to Fontainebleau, only some forty miles southeast of Paris. Twelve years before we had stopped briefly there, but time had permitted us only a fleeting glimpse of the park in which the palace is located—enough to convince us that these magnificent grounds deserved a return visit. The second time around exceeded even our high expectations.

One of the largest of the royal residences in France, the palace dates to the twelfth century when Louis VII stayed in the original chateau. For hundreds of years monarchs and heads of state have favored

Fontainebleau as a retreat from Paris. Francis I built the horseshoe-shaped Cour Ovale, the central part of the sprawling palace complex. Other monarchs who enjoyed this setting and contributed additions to the palace and gardens were Louis IX (Saint Louis), Henri IV, Louis XIII, Napoleon I, Louis XVIII, Louis Philippe and Napoleon III. Even Louis XIV, although preoccupied with the building of Versailles, made visits nearly every year to Fontainebleau, and it was here that he revoked the Edict of Nantes in 1685.

The palace sits on the edge of a two-hundred-acre park, one of France's most beautiful wooded tracts. Those monarchs fond of hunting found this forest an ideal setting for their sport. Nearly all of the royal palaces boasted large hunting preserves, and the movement of royal courts from palace to palace was dictated in part by hunting opportunities. A more mundane and practical consideration also necessitated such moves. Sanitation in the royal residences was as primitive as the decoration was grand. Human waste along with kitchen waste often went directly into the moats or other nearby bodies of water. In time the health conditions and the stench became unbearable, and the court had to move on to new places.

On our second visit to Fontainebleau our time was again limited, and we had to choose between touring the inside or strolling through the vast gardens around the palace. Glorious sunshine and Suzanne's longing to tour the gardens decided the issue for us. On this weekday in October we saw no more than five or six other visitors. First we walked through the English garden with its ancient and enormous plane trees, pines, and cypress scattered about in the seemingly haphazard manner of English landscaper Capability Brown.

After passing through the Jardin de Diane with its handsome fountain depicting the Goddess of the Hunt, her hounds, and the heads of the hunted stags, we arrived at the great expanse of the Grand Parterre. This formal space manages to achieve a sense of intimacy and charm far greater than that of Versailles even though it was laid out in its final form by Le Nôtre. Under his direction the Tibre river was diverted to form a large basin, one of the main features of the garden. S. admired especially the long mixed borders punctuated at regular intervals with bold clumps of miscanthus grass.

We dined in an attractive one-star restaurant across from the entrance to the palace, Le Beauharnais, in the hotel named for Napoleon's striking symbol, L'Aigle Noir (the Black Eagle). An unusual footnote on their menu which appealed to us was a suggestion for those with smaller appetites to order only a couple of courses (an entrée and a plat or a plat and dessert) rather than the typical multicourse dinner. We took the suggestion and chose as an entrée a delightful seafood *pot au feu* of scallops and leeks. As we expected in an upscale restaurant, we were presented first off with a trio of small pre-entrée goodies, the amuse-gueules assurance of good things to come. Napoleon perhaps would have wanted heartier fare, but for us the dinner was just right!

Rue St-Antoine, Marais

*I*n October 1996 we struck out for new terrain—a rental apartment on the right bank of the Seine in the Marais only a short walk from our beloved Ile St-Louis, but a world apart in atmosphere. This apartment was highly recommended by a friend who had rented it previously. The proprietor, a Washingtonian, spends several months each year in the apartment. The photographs and literature she provided assured us that the apartment, though very small, would suit our needs. A clever architectural renovation has converted the space into very livable quarters with all the necessities tucked in compactly. Simple modern furniture and a few older pieces complement

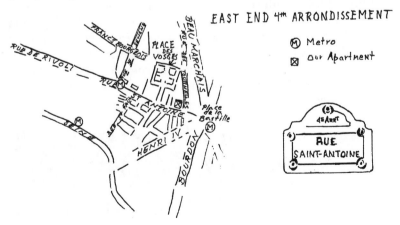

EAST END 4ᵗʰ ARRONDISSEMENT

Ⓜ Metro
⊠ Our Apartment

the all white decor. Entry off the street through a high-gloss cobalt blue door into a quiet and spacious courtyard with greenery in planters was a welcome contrast to the noisy traffic on rue St-Antoine.

This street, an extension of rue de Rivoli running east to the Place Bastille, is one of the oldest thoroughfares of Paris. Today it is lined by a hodgepodge of typical Parisian food shops along with some ethnic eateries and a mix of boutiques ranging from cut-rate to upscale. These occupy the lower floors of former private houses now mostly made into apartments. The entire Marais is caught up in a surge of gentrification.

While most observers regard the renovation of the Marais as a positive example of urban renewal, some critics, alarmed at the loss of architectural relics of the past, have stoutly opposed the process. In 1965 a government edict zoned the district for special protection and banned renovations that changed its character. Contemporary swings in the fortunes of the Marais are only the latest in the up and down history of this part of Paris.

In the twelfth century the Knights Templars and other religious orders began clearing the land and erecting isolated monasteries and churches. Gradually settlers took up farming and sent their produce to markets in Paris. A defining moment came in 1605 when Henri IV commissioned the building of the Place Royale on what was then a large field and gave the lots facing the square to 36 noblemen on condition that they build identical mansions on all four sides. The project was a grander version of the one Henri had initiated at Place Dauphine. Now, nearly four centuries later in the Marais these stone and brick houses with slate roofs and high chimneys enclose one of Europe's oldest and most charming squares, renamed the Place des Vosges. The covered arcade at ground level of each house provided a sheltered walkway to protect the finery of the original wealthy occupants. Today it serves the eager visitors who come to enjoy shopping in the boutiques and galleries or dining in the several restaurants and bistros around the square.

Having been the center of fashionable Paris where many wealthy citizens settled in pre-revolutionary Paris, the area plunged into neglect and partial decay after the Revolution. Deserted by the fashionable and powerful families, it became a center of artisans and craftsmen. Today the Marais is back in vogue while many of the displaced artisans carry on their traditional trades wherever they can find affordable spaces near their old haunts.

HÔTEL DE SULLY

Our apartment was only steps away from the Hôtel de Sully, the best preserved of all the mansions facing on Place des Vosges. During daylight hours the public can walk through the ground level of this house, entering either from the square or through the grand portal on rue St. Antoine. History buffs will remember that Henri II was killed here accidentally in a jousting tournament in 1559, and his widow Catherine de Medici persuaded her son to demolish the palace where the tournament was held. That palace was on the site of the Hôtel de Sully built in the early seventeenth century.

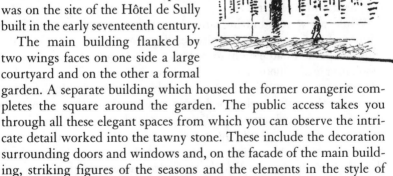

The main building flanked by two wings faces on one side a large courtyard and on the other a formal garden. A separate building which housed the former orangerie completes the square around the garden. The public access takes you through all these elegant spaces from which you can observe the intricate detail worked into the tawny stone. These include the decoration surrounding doors and windows and, on the facade of the main building, striking figures of the seasons and the elements in the style of Rubens. The upper floors of this great house are not open to the public.

In 1965 the Hôtel de Sully was designated as headquarters of the National Office of Historic Monuments and Sites. That office, which manages over one hundred state-owned chateaux and other important monuments in all parts of France, provides visitors with literature and information on visiting their properties.

VICTOR HUGO MUSEUM

Between 1832 and 1848 Victor Hugo lived in an elegant apartment on the third floor of another house on Place des Vosges. Early in the twentieth century the entire building was converted into a museum honoring one of France's most illustrious men of letters. It contains a remarkable collection of Hugo's effects—furniture, paintings and other artifacts demonstrating his great range of talents. Suzanne and I were expecting memorabilia relating to his prolific writing and were astounded to see examples of his handiwork as painter and interior decorator—watercolors, painted chests and wall panels carved and decorated with amusing designs and cartoons. Hugo was an inveterate collector of antiques and bric-a-brac from different periods which he enjoyed mixing together.

Hugo's times and his tempestuous life come into vivid reality as you tour the museum. In this apartment he and his wife raised their four children while he was writing works such as *Ruy Blas* and *Les Misérables*. After failing four times to be elected to the French Academy, he was finally accepted in 1841. In addition he became increasingly active in politics. He vacillated between a leaning towards monarchy with the trappings of imperial power and the libertarian views for which he is best known. His advocacy of liberal causes such as universal suffrage led to his banishment from France and his exile during which he lived mostly on the Isle of Guernsey before a triumphant return to Paris.

While we were admiring Hugo's imaginative wall panels in the Chinese drawing room, I was also reading aloud to Suzanne from the museum guide I had bought on entering. It referred several times to a woman named Juliette Drouet. As we were trying to figure out her connection to Hugo, a young man in a white coat on a ladder touching up one of the wall panels piped up in excellent English to inform us that she was Hugo's mistress. Not content with furnishing this information, he went on to tell how it was customary for Frenchmen at the age of about forty to acquire a mistress and often to keep her, as Hugo did, close to the family. Finally he added knowingly that the same practice continues today in France, though no doubt not in the United States. We indicated that even stranger things happen in the United States, and thanked him for his helpful insights.

• • •

Le Viaduc des Arts

Not far from this apartment is an outstanding example of an old building put to new use—the Viaduc des Arts, an eight-block viaduct built originally in the reign of Napoleon III as support for a railway. On Avenue Daumesnil behind the Opéra Bastille this long abandoned structure was transformed with great imagination about five years ago into a series of *ateliers* for artisans. The project was undertaken at the initiative of then-mayor of Paris Jacques Chirac. What used to be an eyesore that had long outlived its original purpose is now a pleasing row of commodious light-filled spaces where skilled craftsmen produce and sell their wares. The original graceful arches of the old viaduct have been enclosed by glass to form some thirty workplaces that double as showrooms for a remarkable variety of products. Creative designs of practical items such as fireplace mantles, kitchen counters, bathroom fixtures, mirrors, iron furniture, fountains, and gilt picture frames, coexist with workshops featuring jewelry, leather clothing, and paintings. The shops, which seem to cater more to wholesale buyers than to the general public, were doing a brisk business on the day of our visit.

When we spotted an intriguing sign for a stairway leading to a *Promenade Planté* (a planted walkway), we climbed to the top to find a beautifully landscaped brick walk stretching the entire eight-block length of the viaduct. Suzanne thought she had gone to heaven when she took in the long stretch of magnificent planting on either side of the walk. Expertly pruned and maintained, the imaginative planting scheme included low ground cover in front of evergreens, small trees and masses of white roses still in bloom. One section featured bamboo ranging from dwarf to very tall. Three stories above ground level, the promenade offered panoramic views of the surrounding area. We descended on another stairway that led one flight down to a brick-paved square from which you could look through the tops of the arches into the the artists' studios.

On mentioning our discovery to some of our Paris friends, none had ever heard of it. But the project deserves special praise because it transforms an ugly architectural duckling into a swan and, in the process, creates spaces for the artisans who have formed the entrepreneurial backbone of this part of Paris over the centuries.

The restored viaduct stands in sharp contrast to its nearby neighbor, the controversial Opéra Bastille. The only positive attributes of this architectural horror are its reported good acoustics, the comfortable seats in its large auditorium, and its brilliant appearance at night. By day, however, its enormous expanses of ugly opaque glass, white marble and gray granite are visually repellent. To add to the sense of aesthetic injury, the crumbling exterior masonry has posed such a danger to passersby that the walls have had to be covered with netting. Alas, it seems that this huge ugly hulk will be a blight on the urban landscape long into the future.

CULINARY VENTURES

During this week we returned to several favorite restaurants, Le Petit Laurent, l'Orangerie, Guirlande de Julie, and the Café Marly. It's fun to revisit places you've enjoyed before, and we came away each time with our initial judgments reinforced. Furthermore our assessments of these four very different restaurants have been confirmed in subsequent press reviews. Another dining reprieve was a delightful evening with Polly Platt, author of *French or Foe?* and her husband at their apartment. Polly managed to find the time in her busy schedule to prepare a great dinner featuring a delicious pasta dish as the main course.

Two restaurants near our apartment that we did *not* visit deserve mention because they are famous and popular. First is Ambroisie in the Place des Vosges, one of only twenty restaurants in all of France with three Michelin stars. Undoubtedly we would have adored the classic cuisine and intimate dining room, if our budget had allowed it. The second spot, Bofinger, one of the oldest brasseries in Paris and designated a national landmark, is affordable and always crowded. But its great size and its reputation as a place to see and be seen do not appeal to us. We chose instead the much smaller and cozier Bistrot du Dôme (one fork) across the street from Bofinger where we enjoyed a good seafood dinner.

The Marais has a number of wine bars, the informal eating and drinking places that came into vogue several years ago. We chose one cited in a review we had read before leaving the States. It was full almost to capacity and we were scrunched into a tiny space at the top of stairs to the kitchen. It was obviously an "in" place for the mixed clientele, but not one that we would want to visit soon again. We were disappointed by the mediocre fare and undistinguished wine. Later we heard that we would have been better off at some of the other wine bars in our area. The wine bar phenomenon strikes us as a fad somewhat like the current mania in the U.S. for coffee bars. Paris wine bars cater to a wide variety of clienteles from well-to-do professionals to manual workers and shop keepers. Men tend to be their principal customers, though women are certainly in evidence. The female counterpart of the wine bar is the *salon de thé* where light lunches are served and alcohol is not offered. Though the Ile St-Louis teahouse depicted in my painting has gone out of business, such establishments continue to meet a need in most local neighborhoods. Hard as it is to believe, Paris now has more tea salons than London.

On the same street as the wine bar where we lunched, the rue du Bourg-Tibourg, is a remarkable establishment called Mariage Frères, a Maison de Thé established in 1854. The founders were tea connoisseurs exasperated by the poor quality of leaves available in Great Britain. This is a shop where serious tea drinkers can select from among over five hundred of the world's most highly prized teas, some astronomically priced. A staff of white-linen-coated tea experts guides customers among the shelves of tea canisters carefully labeled for provenance and proper serving in accordance with tea-drinking ritual. A small restaurant allows customers to sample their selections with the appropriate food. Even for those who are not tea aficionados this emporium in well worth a visit.

CROSS-CURRENTS IN THE SEAS OF PARISIAN CUISINE

Keeping up with the trends in Parisian cuisine, while it can be fun and fascinating, can also be baffling and exasperating. Even informed patrons trying to be *au courant* about what's happening can become confused by the swings in food fashions and the impassioned, sometimes belligerent, hype of would-be trend-setters. Parisian cuisine is in a state of flux not unlike the chaotic state of *haute couture*. Always looming over the culinary wars is the trauma of the Michelin star awards. The rankings by Gault Millau and Hachette, though each of these guides has a loyal following, rarely stir as much controversy. But changes at the upper levels of Michelin rankings generate a degree of media frenzy equaled only by major contests in the football leagues. Advocates of a particular chef can become apoplectic if their favorite loses a star or one of his rivals gains one.

The public sense of discontent emerging in these "Star Wars" stems in no small part from the Olympian attitude of Michelin which does not deign to explain its reasoning. But their decisions can spell either fame and fortune or professional and financial ruin. It seems that great creative talent in the kitchen is not always accompanied by sound financial judgment, and several master chefs have gone bankrupt through extravagant outlays for a distinctive ambiance to impress the Michelin representatives as well as customers.

Recent years have seen a major struggle between purists seeking to preserve the Frenchness of their cuisine and the so-called "fusion" school welcoming foreign cuisines to Paris. One of the most bally-hooed Parisian chefs currently is Pierre Gagnaire. His three-star restaurant offering Asian-influenced dishes, some of which featured the entrails of chickens and pigeons, went bankrupt in 1996, but, undaunted, he reopened another eponymous restaurant in the eighth arrondissement which now enjoys a reputation for chic and three stars in the latest Michelin. Known as the master of Mystery Meats, Gagnaire said in 1993 "Nothing makes me happier than hearing people say 'I have no idea what I ate but it sure was good.'"

Strongly opposed to these foreign influences are such classic French cuisine master chefs as Joel Robuchon and his successor, Alain Ducasse at the ultra fashionable restaurant (three stars, four red forks) bearing his name in an elegant Belle Epoque townhouse in the sixteenth arrondissement. These two chefs were among the principal organizers, along with Georges Blanc, head of the Federation of French *Haute Cuisine*, of a 1996 proclamation extolling the virtues of French regional cuisine and condemning the practice of combining anything and everything on one plate for the sake of innovation. This proclamation provoked a counterattack by non-traditionalist chefs denouncing the old guard as "obsolete, unrealistic, and dangerous." The French flair for disputation over matters which outside of France would not seem of transcendental consequence appears to be fully intact.

Robuchon won the third star for his restaurant in 1984 by working eighteen hour days beginning with predawn calls to suppliers and ending only when the last customers had consumed their liqueurs. Unwilling to continue this stressful existence and wanting to quit when he was ahead, Robuchon retired at the age of fifty-one. Ducasse has already expressed his intention to follow his mentor's example. But now, in his early forties, he is too busily caught up in his quest for celebrity. A frenetic triangular commute takes him, often by helicopter, from his Paris restaurant to another three star restaurant in Monte Carlo and thence to a country inn in Moustiers. His Paris restaurant won a favorable review in the *New York Times* by a reviewer who felt he was privileged to pay $528 for a splendid dinner for three. However, *La Belle France* called it the biggest disappointment of the year; the cuisine was too expensive and "just plain dull." But Ducasse is the only French chef who can boast a total of six stars.

Many of the better-known chefs in Paris have started less expensive and simpler spin-offs of their upscale restaurants. Robuchon in his retirement oversees several such establishments sometimes called "designer bistros." (Incidentally, the word "bistro" derives from the Russian word for "fast" which is what Russian troops shouted to French waiters when they were stationed in Paris after the Napoleonic wars.)

Among culinary authorities Robuchon is known as the exponent of freshness and simplicity. He insists that all the ingredients, notably vegetables and fruits but also dairy products and staples, be fresh. If fresh asparagus is not available in the market, it does not appear on the menu. Secondly, he advocates what he calls *cuisine actuelle*, which seeks to maximize the true flavor of whatever is being cooked rather than disguising that flavor with seasoning or sauces. His philosophy has influenced all aspects of French cuisine from the great restaurants to the humbler establishments.

Amid the explosion of new bistros many older ones are thriving. Often they are family-run operations that have been in business for a long while. Their place in Parisian gastronomy is assured by *prix fixe* menus with lower prices than those of the better restaurants and by the fact that many diners today are seeking simpler fare and more casual atmosphere. To keep prices down some bistros now feature odd cuts such as beef cheeks, ox tails and calves' tongues. Traditionally bistros used to offer homely standbys such as *pot au feu, coq au vin, and boeuf bourgignon*. An example of an old bistro favorite that still holds a place on today's menus is the potato pancake. Following is Suzanne's easy-does-it recipe:

POTATO AND CHIVES PANCAKES *serves six*
(POMMES DE TERRE ET CIBOULETTES EN CRÈPE)

6 medium boiling potatoes
1 bunch chives
unsalted butter, salt, and pepper

Peel potatoes, then grate or shred (should make three cups). Blot dry
with dish towel. In a heavy skillet heat two tablespoons butter, add ½
cup shredded potatoes, distributing evenly to cover entire surface.
Tamp down firmly. Sprinkle with snipped chives, salt and pepper.
Cook over medium heat until underside is golden. Turn pancake, add
more butter as needed, again sprinkling with chives, salt and pepper,
cook until golden. Keep pancakes warm in oven until serving.

Though such staples still retain a place on many bistro menus,
nowadays they may be less prominently featured than specialty dishes
adapted by the chef from other cuisines such as the Mediterranean or
Provencal. Patricia Wells, the highly regarded food critic of the
International Herald Tribune cited four of the most popular of these
bistros in a *New York Times* article, La Verrière, L'Affriole, Chez
Michel, and Les Olivades. Each with its distinctive culinary personality and ambiance, has achieved great popularity. Despite their relatively low prices, their increasingly sophisticated menus suggest that they
are part of a counter-current pulling some bistros toward the world of
haute cuisine.

One of the most expensive bistros where reserving a table is next to
impossible is L'Ami Louis which opened in 1930 and has adamantly
retained its shabbiness ever since. Its devotees are happy to pay a high
tab for thick slices of foie gras and other dishes slathered in goose fat.
Thus this nearly fifty-year-old institution flies directly in the face of
two major trends on the Paris restaurant scene, the one being reduced
fat in the diet, the other being dressed-up decor.

All over the city and especially in outlying areas ethnic bistros offer
exotic foods based on cuisines of Africa, Asia and Latin America. The
casual atmosphere of these bistros contrasts sharply with older established ethnic restaurants such as Tan Dinh, a favorite of ours in the seventh arrondissement serving fine Vietnamese cuisine. We have also
enjoyed several dinners at Lao Tseu, a Chinese restaurant in Sylvie's
neighborhood on the Boulevard St-Germain. If you are seeking a particular kind of ethnic food, you wil find it in the red Michelin list of

Spécialités étrangères in front of the pages on Paris or in a special section of Gault-Millau.

Still another wave in Paris gastronomy is the appearance of what the French call *nourriture bio*, organic foods grown without chemicals. This movement stems partly from rising environmental awareness on the part of Parisians who are becoming concerned about urban pollution and its effects on personal well-being. The best-known open market for such products is located on Boulevard Raspail in the sixth arrondissement. In addition, a three-year-old mini-chain of *supermarchés bio* offers a large choice of organic foods (eighty different kinds of grains in open barrels, for example) in low-tech surroundings. Some of these organic food products are offered in the many health food stores all over Paris.

The growing interest in health foods in Paris comes at a time when experts are reporting a previously little known disparity in the overall health and life expectancy between northern and southern (or Mediterranean) France. Statistics now show that, in the south where red wine with meals is common and where cooking is done with olive oil and vegetable oil rather than butter and animal fats, average life expectancy is as much as five years longer than in the north. It seems then that the famous *paradoxe français* is really a phenomenon of southern France where people's eating habits resemble those of their Italian or Spanish neighbors.

With so many currents and cross-currents in Parisian cuisine who knows where it is heading? In the eyes of this beholder, at any rate, it becomes harder even to draw a clear line between restaurants, bistros, cafés, brasseries and wine bars. Rather than trying to keep up with each new fad or seeking out the latest "in" establishment, Suzanne and I follow our own tastes, enjoy our old favorites along with an occasional new place, while allowing the Parisians to sort out for themselves their obsession with the art of the table.

AU REVOIR MARAIS

Our week in the Marais was the windup of three weeks spent in France. Although we were ready to return to Washington, we were leaving Paris with great regret and the gnawing sense that, once again, we needed more time. Paris requires a lifetime, and we give it only one week a year. But the memories are with us all through the year as is the expectation of returning next year.

Allô Marais, Nous Voici Encore!

*H*appily, we did indeed return in October 1997 and back to the same apartment we'd rented the year before. This time we came to Paris via Eurostar through the Chunnel from England where we had spent a couple of weeks. What struck us most about the experience was the extent to which the Chunnel has succeeded in linking the people of Britain and the Continent after millenia of physical separation. Londoners think nothing of zipping across to Paris for a day of shopping and dining, while the reverse holds true for Parisians. The ease of traveling back and forth will surely strengthen the economies of the countries on both ends of the Chunnel as well as the cultural bonds. After all the doubts raised by skeptics of this ambitious and costly project it is gratifying to see how well it works.

On arriving at the Gare du Nord we spent over a half hour in a long queue of other baggage-laden travelers waiting for taxis. And when finally ensconced in a cab heading to our apartment we were delayed by a *manifestation*, (they seem to occur with increasing regularity) and the driver had to snake his way on a circuitous route to the Marais. But once we had pulled up to the familiar blue door of our building, we felt altogether at home and thrilled to be there. Being a bit travel worn and wanting to unpack, call our friends, and settle into our apartment, we elected not to dine out but have a simple dinner at home. Shopping for dinner and other items needed for our week's stay was simplified by the presence of a small supermarket almost directly across the street.

Along with feeling at home came another new sensation, an awareness that, although we had by no means exhausted the points of interest in the vast Paris metropolis, we had seen enough not to feel the need to cram every day with sightseeing. We had already made reservations by FAX for three restaurant dinners, and we felt entitled to relax and enjoy *la vie Parisienne*. This is not to say that we stayed home watching TV. Indeed we made two forays to places we had not seen, places as widely separated in space and time as anything Paris has to offer; the Cluny Museum (actually called *Musée National du Moyen Age/Thermes de Cluny*) and La Défense. The Cluny, located on the site of second and third century Gallo-Roman baths, is housed in a mansion of the abbots of Cluny dating to 1480, and contains an unsurpassed collection of medieval art. In the greatest possible contrast, La Défense is the huge high-tech city of the future appended to Paris on its northwest perimeter.

HÔTEL DE CLUNY

For our visit to this museum and other sites in the Latin Quarter we arranged a walking tour with Sheila Hallsted who had guided us on our visit to Montmartre. Her impressive academic credentials in French history include a doctoral dissertation on the history of the Paris Metro system.

We walked first to the Roman baths, a collection of high-walled spaces; one wall reaching up an incredible forty-six feet.

Made of alternating layers of brick and rubble remarkably preserved, the walls separate what were the cold, lukewarm, and hot bathing rooms of a public bath house. The barbarians sacked this compound in the third century, and it was abandoned until about 1330 when the Abbot of the influential Burgundian Cluny order bought the site in order to build a splendid residence for himself and other abbots visiting the college they founded near the Sorbonne. In contrast to the austere architecture of the the order's monasteries, this residence was built in magnificent Flamboyant Gothic style, richly embellished with the symbols of ecclesiastical power. It was one of the earliest examples of a hôtel particulier, really a château, in the city. In the seventeenth century it served as residence of the papal nuncio, Cardinal Mazarin. During the Revolution it was sold for the benefit of the state to be used by a series of owners who covered up the baths with six feet of soil to make vegetable gardens and an orchard.

The salvation of the entire complex came in 1833 when a wealthy collector of medieval art, Alexandre Du Sommerard bought it and installed his vast collection and supervised the site's restoration until his death in 1842. Rarely has one man done as much to preserve historical heritage. The state acquired the property on his death and soon afterwards opened it as a museum.

The treasures inside are rich beyond belief. Most important are the famous tapestries of the lady and the unicorn, six perfectly preserved hangings in an upstairs rotunda. The purity and intensity of colors and the intricate design (uniform red backgrounds, brilliant blue-green floral designs, and wondrous mythical creatures joining the unicorn to pay homage to their noble lady) are breathtaking. Several other tapestry series are displayed in other rooms along with illuminated manuscripts, stained glass medallions from Sainte-Chapelle, ivories, a splendid gold altar frontal from Basle Cathedral, to mention only some of the principal artworks. Another important collection consists of fragments of sculpture originally from Notre-Dame, including twenty-one heads from the King's gallery dating to the twelfth and thirteenth century. Because the museum collection is so eclectic and the signage leaves much to be desired, one should take a guided tour and allow most of a half day for the visit.

From the Cluny we walked up the hill to the Sorbonne and into its great interior courtyard. At one end is the imposing domed church commissioned by Cardinal Richelieu when he was in charge of the

college. His tomb, said to be the finest example of French funerary sculpture of the seventeenth century, is designed in the form of an altar. The church is opened only rarely, sometimes for exhibits of contemporary art. After passing through one of the main corridors of the nineteenth century main college building, we went out to the side from which one can see the astronomy tower, the first-ever incorporated in a university.

Sheila made a point of correcting the common misconception of the Sorbonne as the ultimate pinnacle of the French educational system. Indeed she likened it more to one of our state universities, representing only a step on the road to higher education at one of the truly elite institutions—the Ecole Polytechnique founded by Napoleon to train military officers and considered the most difficult engineering school in the world, the Ecole Nationale d'Administration (ENA) to train senior civil servants, or one of the several other select engineering graduate schools. Another academic institution Sheila showed us from the outside was the College de France founded by François Premier in 1530. This unorthodox part of the university system awards no degrees, recruits teachers regardless of their academic credentials, and frequently serves as a center of opposition to the establishment.

Walking further up what was once known as "the sacred hill of pagan Lutetia" we passed by the Clovis Tower and the Church of St-Etienne du Mont about the same age as St-Germain-des-Prés, and entered the great square surrounding the Pantheon. Sheila told us about the architectural evolution of the building into its present monumental form based on the plan of the Greek cross with the multi-columned portico borrowed from the Pantheon in Rome.

Outings with Sheila are a very informative and enjoyable means to see and learn about Paris. The challenge is always to retain the tremendous amount of data she provides. At lunch in a café below the Pantheon we had a chance to shift from past to present, catching up on each other's news and Sheila's new role as mother.

La Défense

Until this year we had avoided La Défense, though I was less opposed to going there than Suzanne who imagined it as a forbidding and dehumanizing collection of brutal architectural structures. While our visit served to slightly modify her preconception, it changed me

into an advocate. We both applaud the zoning policies which restrict the building of skyscrapers within the city, so the rationale for siting La Défense on the outskirts of Paris is uncontestable. But I was much more taken than S. with the stunning architectural statements made by the diverse buildings comprising this huge modern city as well as the layout of the entire complex. It breaks away altogether from the traditional style of Parisian architecture, yet pays respect to that style by its focus on the vista of the Paris cityscape. The Grande Arche, as noted earlier, stands at the western end of "the great axis" running from the Louvre Arc du Carousel and passing through the Arc de Triomphe.

We took an easy and rapid metro trip on Line 1 which ends at La Défense. The below ground level is almost a city in itself with shops, services, galleries, and miles of passages linking all systems of transport, but it does involve some long walks between station stops. Once you emerge above ground and have your first look at the Grande Arche, you can hardly believe what your eyes are telling you. A colossal cube with a hole in the middle big enough to accommodate the facade of Notre-Dame with space to spare. On one side are the external elevators that take you to the top of the arch and offer views of Paris and the complex of La Défense as you ascend or descend.

After obtaining tickets for the ride in the glass-enclosed elevator we joined other tourists and watched as the ground below us receded. On stepping out at the top floor, we were pleasantly surprised to find a huge exhibition space featuring contemporary sculpture and paintings of French artists from around the Francophone world. We were especially drawn to the slender, graceful carved wooden works of a Senegalese artist, but there were many other appealing and innovative pieces well displayed in a series of large exhibit spaces. Quite a few of the works were light-hearted and amusing, while none were ugly or depressing. These artists were obviously well trained, highly skilled, and focused on positive visual impressions in contrast with the in-your-face shock treatment of so many contemporary American artists and galleries.

We lunched at Le Jardin, a small restaurant next to the exhibition in a round enclosure screened off from the surrounding space. Here we were able to enjoy a perfectly adequate and inexpensive meal while we discussed what we had seen so far and what we might do next. We examined the small illustrated map of La Défense given us with our tour tickets. The map identifies each of the many offices, residential buildings, parks, and recreational areas in the city.

Even Suzanne, the skeptic, had to admit that the overall concept succeeds in achieving its purpose, providing a central location for both public agencies and private companies engaged in the high-technology enterprises of the military/industrial complex. Its planners deserve credit not only for sparing the city of Paris the intrusion of high-rise complexes which could never have fitted into the Paris cityscape, but also for creating a new habitat for the future. Critics point out that the office space in the Grande Arche itself still has many vacancies and remains a white elephant. The space is expensive, and it competes with the many corporate office buildings located nearby. But the building itself does make a compelling and, for me anyway, fascinating architectural statement.

What I admire most about the concept of La Défense is that it helps to minimize urban and suburban sprawl in what remains of the country surrounding Paris which, Lord knows, is in need of protection. City and regional planning in France has far greater acceptance than in the United States, with the result that the countryside around towns and cities is more effectively preserved. Anyone who has driven in the French provinces will agree that this is one of the appeals of France, in contrast to the haphazard spread of malls and sprawling developments in America. In France you are far more likely to find a sharp demarcation between a city or town and the surrounding countryside. La Défense should be commended for confining growth in a single location.

On my next visit to Paris I intend to revisit La Défense to see all that I missed on this occasion, whether with or without Suzanne, who knows? On this day, because it had begun to rain, we skipped a walk after our descent from the Grande Arche and went underground to pick up the #73 bus straight to a convenient stop at Concorde.

RECONNECTING WITH MY LONG-LOST PARIS NEPHEW

On our earlier visits to Paris I had always tried without success to contact my nephew Jean Pierre Szabo, a native Parisian whom I had not seen for some thirty years. Because JP, as he is called in the family, spends more time in his house in the Pyrenees than in Paris, I could never reach him. This year, however, with advance warning, JP arranged to come to Paris while we were there.

A graduate in architecture of the Ecole des Beaux Arts, JP was intrigued by our interest in the Parisian cityscape for which he has a keen appreciation. After meeting us in our apartment he led us on a walk through areas of historic interest in the Marais, La Cité, and Ile St-Louis. He pointed out some of the oldest buildings on narrow streets such as rue François Miron where fourteenth century regulations had required the fronts to recede to allow sunlight to reach street level. He also showed us how the little stone bollards regularly spaced close to the houses were designed so that pedestrians could stand between them to avoid being run over by speeding carriages.

We paused for a while in front of the Hôtel de Sens near the Seine, which along with the Hôtel de Cluny, is one of the few remaining residences built during the Middle Ages. JP focused his remarks on some of the distinguishing features of the Gothic porch and turrets, while lamenting some of the more recent restoration.

Our photograph on the jacket of this book is one of many taken by JP on our walk. So that we could see them without delay, he had his film developed in one of the many one-hour photo shops found all over central Paris.

We lunched at one of our perennial favorites on the Place des Vosges, the Guirlande de Julie. In the all too brief span of a luncheon conversation JP and I caught up on three decades and vowed that we would stay in close touch from now on.

OTHER DINING EXPERIENCES

As noted earlier, we had made three restaurant reservations by FAX before leaving Washington, including the dinner at the Jules Verne, where tables must be booked very far in advance. The other two restaurants were old favorites, Le Petit Laurent and the Ferme St-Simon. At the former we were greeted warmly by the maitre d'hôtel on our sixth annual pilgrimage to his establishment. It was a delight to find that nothing had changed in the muted yellow and gray decor or general ambiance. Every table was occupied by diners who seemed mostly to be habitués.

We had booked a table for five at Ferme St-Simon, for we had invited our friend Sylvie along with Polly Platt and Andé. It was fun for us to introduce Parisians who had never met each other but lived not far apart and shared common interests and an attachment to this particular restaurant. Conversation bubbled along throughout dinner which, incidentally, lived up entirely to past standards, despite the unjustified removal of the Michelin star. Neither Polly, Andé or Sylvie knew of the removal of the star, and did not seem to care.

We were all riveted to Sylvie's account of her time spent in German-occupied Paris. She remembers being always hungry and, during the winter months, always cold. One night in 1943 she and some friends, defying their parents' strict instructions to remain at home, skipped off to Maxim's for dinner. While they were about to begin their second course, they heard the explosions of bombs being dropped nearby and the warning wail of a siren. The bombs were dropped by American planes on the Renault plant being operated by the Nazis. Sylvie and friends hurried to a cellar below Maxim's where they finished the rest of their dinner and then, against all civil defense orders, ran through the pitch dark metro tunnel for four stops until they reached the rue du Bac station.

The story reminded us all of how close Paris came to being burned to the ground in the final days of the occupation. Now, more than fifty years after liberation, many Parisians are reliving that period, caught up in introspection and self-doubt. At the same time France faces graver and more pressing problems as it tries to hold its own in the turmoil of political and economic change in Europe and the rest of the globe. But, just as Paris narrowly escaped the burning ordered by Hitler, so will it come through its present trials. It is too glorious and too beautiful not to survive. The continuing popularity of Paris as a destination for travelers from all over the globe signals the universal and unique appeal of the City of Light.

A BIENTÔT PARIS

Rather than au revoir it's more comforting to say à bientôt, as in "see you soon," because we expect to return for our fifteenth annual visit to Paris and our tenth apartment rental. Though we will still be tourists, we will be more familiar with what Paris has to offer and how to fashion a temporary home from a tiny apartment. For a brief interlude we will come close to living an enchanted *vie Parisienne*.

How You Can Find the
Right Apartment for Your Budget

*T*he decision to rent an apartment rather than staying in a hotel obviously involves some significant trade-offs. As noted in an excellent article on apartment renting in *La Belle France*, a newsletter cited in Appendix C, renting requires a good deal more work than reserving a room in a hotel. Information on hotels is readily available, while apartment rental information requires searching in specialized sources. The following pages are designed to simplify that search.

First-time visitors to Paris, unless they are at ease in the French language and quite daring, may be well-advised to start out in a hotel where their daily needs are more likely to be met by a concierge and staff. Of course, many regular visitors to Paris are unwilling to forego the amenities and comforts of hotel living. The more *grand luxe* the better in the eyes of great numbers of travelers. On the other hand, more and more Americans and other foreigners are lured by the adventure, or the economies, or both that come with apartment renting. Prospective renters, however, should be prepared to settle for *small* spaces (large rental apartments are quite rare) and they should be warned of certain conditions or possible obstacles.

Rental agencies or private apartment owners almost always require a substantial prepayment before putting a hold on an apartment and payment in full one or two months in advance of occupancy. With few exceptions credit cards cannot be used, and all payments must be made by check. Refunds are almost never made for cancellations. Although most of our rentals have not required security deposits, many agencies do require them, and they can range up to several hundred dollars.

Usually they are not refunded for four to eight weeks after vacating the apartment.

Once you have decided to accept the various conditions, there are many different ways to go about renting. To make the most informed decisions you should check out at least some of the considerable literature available in both the U. S. and France on individual apartments and rental agencies. If you are lucky enough to know or have a connection to the owner of a Paris apartment, by all means explore that channel first. Or you may know someone who has already rented who can advise you; word of mouth is always a good way to go. We were fortunate to have the friends who rented us our first apartment on La Cité which we took for a second year. Dealing directly with the owner has the benefit of eliminating an agency commission. Depending on the duration and the rate of the rental, such a saving can be significant. There is also an advantage in renting from an owner who actually uses the apartment, since it will be more fully furnished and equipped than a property used only for rentals.

The Directory at Appendix A is based mainly on a list published by the French Government Tourist Office with branches in New York, Chicago and Beverly Hills. The New York Office is at 444 Madison Avenue, New York, NY 10022 Tel. 212 315 0888; FAX 212 838 7855. This list covers American rental agencies, each with its own selection of rental apartments. Located in many parts of the United States, they can be easily contacted by those wishing to work with an agency in their own area. Some agencies will provide names of satisfied clients, and most have listings in the outskirts of Paris, where prices may be somewhat lower and where you may find less noise and congestion than in the city. As in any type of financial transaction, it pays to do comparison shopping to select what looks best for you.

More and more college alumni magazines are running ads for apartments belonging to or managed by graduates. This source also worked well for us, leading to two of our rentals. Other periodical sources in the United States include:

1. *New York Review of Books*, 250 West 57th Street, New York. NY 10107, Tel (800) 829 5088
2. *FRANCE-AMERIQUE*, A French-language weekly published in collaboration with Le Figaro by Trocadero Publishing, 1560 Broadway, Suite 511, New York, NY 10036-6997, Tel (212) 221-6997, $45 for year's subscription.

3. *FRANCE TODAY, The Journal of French Travel and Culture*, published ten times a year by France Press Inc. 1051 Divisidero St., San Francisco, CA 94115, Tel (415) 921-5100, $39 for year's subscription

The rates for the apartments we have rented have varied widely from $500 to $1,200 a week with an average of about $800. Ads in a recent issue of FRANCE TODAY offered weekly rentals ranging from $285 for a six-floor walk-up attic apartment to $900.

Sources of rental information published in France should not be overlooked, especially if you happen to be in Paris and considering a rental for a future visit. The Office of Tourism at 127 avenue des Champs Elysées, 75008 Paris, publishes a monthly list of short term rental apartments. The Monday issues of Le Monde always carry real estate classifieds including apartment rentals.

An extremely useful free weekly newsletter circulating in the American community in Paris is FUSAC (FRANCE USA Contacts). It is available in places such as the English language book stores, the American churches, and the American University in Paris. This handout of some seventy pages contains information of interest to the English-speaking community including many apartment rental ads, personal notices and announcements of events. To order copies in the United States contact France Contacts, P.O. Box 115, Cooper Station, New York, NY 10276, Tel 212 929 2929, FAX 212 255 5555

A large French commercial real estate firm, ORION, publishes an illustrated sixty-page catalog of rental properties all over France. In Paris they have four modern apartment complexes equipped with modern facilities located at La Défense, Place d'Italie, Les Halles, and Bastille. The latter two are within walking distance of central Paris while the first two would require public or private transportation. These apartments, while not providing the kind of intimate or cozy atmosphere that we look for in rentals, have the advantages of efficiency and relatively lower rates. Contact ORION Réservations, 20 Place D'Italie F 75628 Paris cedex 13.

An agency called Résidences de Tourisme provides apartments, some with kitchens in apartment hotels. Certain hotel-type facilities are also available at additional costs. Prices range from F400 a night for a small studio to F2000 per night for larger apartments. They have six locations in various parts of the city including 35 rue de Berri 75008, Tel 01 43 59 55 55. Two other agencies for apartment hotels are All Logement Temporaire, 4 Pl. de la Chapelle 75018, Tel 01 42 09 00 07 and Paris Bienvenue, 16 rue Médécin 75017, Tel 01 42 12 40 40.

A small firm that concentrates on Ile St-Louis and the older and more centrally located areas is Servissimo, 18 rue Budé 75004 Paris, Tel 01 43 29 03 23.

Weigh the tradeoffs between all the options. Renting through friends or personal connections has the advantage noted above of eliminating commission. But renting through an agency has some advantages. Nearly all the agencies make a point of inspecting their apartments on a regular basis, and you should verify this during your negotiations. Most have extensive professional experience which permits them to draw up fair leases and documentation on all features of the apartment. Insist on complete information on all essential amenities—phones, household appliances, kitchen supplies, linens, size and types of beds, concierge (if one exists), cleaning arrangements, elevators (where applicable) numbers to call in case of emergency, etc. Documentation should include complete information on the neighborhood of the apartment including shopping, restaurants, transportation, public security as well as local tourist attractions. Photographs of the apartment should be provided. Some rental agencies will provide names of prior renters as references.

If you should want to rent for six months or more, you should be aware that a quirk of French law prohibits short-term rental purveyors from renting for more than six months.

The books and guides in Appendix C will help in developing a budget for your time in Paris. Restaurant meals will probably be your largest budget item. The Red Michelin on France contains an entire section on selected Paris hotels and restaurants with price ranges for each, and similar information is included in the Gault-Millau and Hachette guides.

Directory of Rental Agencies

Agencies in the United States Renting Apartments and Houses in France as most recently listed by the French Government Tourist Office (Subject to change)

At Home Abroad
405 East 56th St. Ste. 6H
New York, NY 10022
Tel 212 421 9165
FAX 212 752 1591
Contact: Claire Packman

At Home in France
P O Box 643
Ashland, OR 97520
Tel 541 488 9467
FAX 541 488 9468
Contact: Allyn Kaufman

B&V Associates
140 East 56th Street #4c
New York, NY 10022
Tel 212 688 7526
Tel 800 755 8266
FAX 212 688 9467
Contact: Patrick Bruneau

Barclay International Group
150 East 52nd Street
New York, NY 10022
Tel 212 832 3777
Tel 800 845 6636
FAX 212 753 1139
Contact: Dawn Barclay

British Travel International
P O Box 299
Elkton, VA 22827
Tel 800 327 6097
FAX 540 298 2347
Contact: Ed Konstant

Drawbridge to Europe
5456 Adams Road
Talent, OR 97540
Tel 888 268 1148
FAX 541 512 0978
Contact: Karin Volpert

Europa Let/Tropical Inn Let
92 N. Main Street
Ashland, OR 97520
Tel 541 482 5806
Tel 800 462 4486
FAX 541 482 0660
Contact: Kathy Driskell

Families Abroad
194 Riverside Drive
New York, NY 10025
Tel 718 768 6185
Tel 212 787 2434
FAX 212 799 8734
Contact: Irene Fingerhut

Fine French Properties
4 Meadow Grass Court
Gaithersburg, MD 20878
Tel 301 963 0019
FAX 301 977 9660
Contact: Lorraine Parsons

French Home Rentals
P O Box 82386
Portland, OR 97282
Tel 503 774 8977
FAX 503 774 8977
Contact: Joanne Carlson

Friendly French Immersion
4810 Queen Mary, Ste. 18
Montreal, H3W1W
Tel 800 334 0266
FAX 514 344 6222
Contact: Michael Grynberg

Friends in France
40 East 19th Street, 8th floor
New York, NY 10003
Tel 212 260 9820
FAX 212 228 0576
Contact: Raymond Foux

Global Home Network
1110D Elden Street #205
Herndon, VA 22070
Tel 703 318 7081
Tel 800 528 3549
FAX 703 318 7086
Contact: Carol Barron

Heaven on Hearth
39 Radcliffe Road
Rochester, NY 14617
Tel 716 342 5550
FAX 716 266 1425
Contact: Nancy Marcussi

Hideaways International
767 Islington Street
Porstmouth, NH 03801
Tel 603 430 4433
Tel 800 843 4433
FAX 603 430 4444
Contact: Michael Thiel

Hometours International
P O Box 11503
Knoxville, TN 37939
Tel 423 690 8484
Tel 800 367 4668
Contact: Moti Ben Ami

MetaVoyage
1756 Plymouth Road # 392
Ann Arbor, MI 48105
Tel 313 995 8685
Tel 800 771 4771
FAX 313 995 3484
Contact: Randa Rassoul

Overseas Connection
Long Wharf Promenade
P O Box 26
Sag Harbor, NY 11963
Tel 516 725 9308
Tel 516 725 1805
FAX 516 725 5825
Contact: Alfredo Merat

Paris Sejour Reservation
645 North Michigan Avenue # 638
Chicago, IL 60611
Tel 312 587 7707
FAX 312 587 9887
Contact: Virginie Menage

Prestige Villas Ltd
P O Box 1046
Southport, CT 06490
Tel 203 245 1302
Tel 800 336 0080
FAX 203 254 7261
Contact: Patti Slavin

Property Rentals International
1 Park W. Circle, Ste 108
Midlothian, VA 23113
Tel 800 220 3332
FAX 804 379 2073
Contact: Leah Powell

Provence West Ltd.
P O Box 2105
Evergreen, CO 80437
Tel 303 674 6942
FAX 303 674 8773
Contact: Linda Posson

Rent a Home International
7200 34th Ave. NW
Seattle, WA 98117
Tel 206 789 9379
Tel 800 488 7368
FAX 206 789 9377
Contact: Hilde Freeman

Rent A Vacation Everywhere
135 Meigs Street
Rochester, NY 14607
Tel 716 246 0760
FAX 716 256 2676
Contact: Gloria Gioia

Rental Directories International
2044 Rittenhouse Square #200
Philadelphia, PA 19103
Tel 215 985 4001
FAX 215 985 0323
Contact: Helen London

VHR Worldwide
235 Kensington Ave.
Norwood, NJ 07648
Tel 201 787 9393
Tel 800 633 3284
FAX 201 767 5510
Contact: Lori Gedon

Villas & Apartments Abroad
420 Madison Ave.# 1003
New York, NY 10017
Tel 212 759 1025
Tel 800 433 3020
FAX 212 755 8316
Contact: S. Delavaille Jones

Villas International
605 Market Street
San Francisco, CA 94105
Tel 415 281 0910
Tel 800 221 2260
FAX 415 281 0919
Contact: David Kendall

Villas of Distinction
P O Box 55
Armonk, NY 10504
Tel 914 273 3331
Tel 800 289 0900
FAX 914 273 3387
Contact: R. Eastman

Ville et Village
2124 Kittredge Street #200
Berkeley, CA 94704
Tel 510 559 8080
FAX 510 559 8217
Contact: Carolyn Grots

WIMCO
P O Box 1461
Newport, RI 02840
Tel 401 849 8012
Tel 800 932 3222
FAX 401 847 6290
Contact: Barclay Warburton

Checklist of Tips for Renters

$\mathcal{T}$his is an abbreviated list of tips that may be helpful to renters. Many apartment owners will provide more detailed lists. Renters will be well-advised to acquire one of the guides cited in the appendix on suggested reading unless one is available in the apartment.

EMERGENCY PHONE NUMBERS AND ADDRESSES

American Embassy, 01 43 12 22 22; 2 av. Gabriel

American Hospital of Paris 01 46 41 25 25; 63 bd Victor-Hugo; 92200 Neuilly-sur-Seine, 24 hour English-speaking emergency service

British Hospital 01 46 39 22 22; 3 rue Barbés, 92300 Levallois

Swann Rocher Pharmacy (Pharmacie Anglo-Americaine) 01 42 60 72 96; 6 rue Castiglione, 1st arrt. The only Paris pharmacy where an English-language prescription will be translated and filled in equivalent medicine. (Most drugstores on the Champs Elysée and Boulevard St-Germain are open around the clock.)

British and American Pharmacy, 01 47 42 49 40; 1 rue Auber 75009

Police 17 or 01 53 71 53 71/73

Fire Department 18

Ambulance SAMU 15 (open daily 24 hours)

S.O.S. Crisis Line 01 47 23 80 80 (Open daily 3 pm -11 pm in English)

Office of Tourism 01 49 52 53 54; 127, av. Des Champs Elysées, 8th arrt. A helpful 24-hour hot line in English is reached at 01 49 52 53 56. The Tourist Office provides maps, guidebooks, train and bus schedules, literature on points of interest in and outside of Paris, lists of agencies offering walking tours, etc. Branch offices are located at the Eiffel Tower and in train stations.

BABYISITTERS

Ababa 01 45 49 46 46; 8, av. Du Maine 15th arrt. Closed Sunday
  (Screened sitters)
Bébé Cool 01 45 04 27 14; 4, rue Faustin Hélie 16th arrt. Closed Sunday
  (Screened sitters)

BIKE RENTALS AND BIKE ROUTES

Paris Vélos-Rent a Bike 01 43 37 59 22; 2 rue du Fer-à-Moulin, 5th arrt.
  Closed October to April

In addition to bike tracks in the Bois de Boulogne and the Bois de Vincennes three recently built bike tracks run from 1) Place de Catalogne, rue Vercingetorix, to Porte de Vanves, 2) from Place d'Italie to rue Jeanne d'Arc, and 3) from Cité des Sciences et de l'Industrie to Quai d'Allier. A cycling organization at 01 48 87 60 01 provides information on bicycle routes with minimum traffic in local districts of Paris.

BOATS

Bateaux-Mouches 01 42 25 96 10; Pont de l'Alma, Right Bank, 8th arrt.
  Very large river cruisers with departures from 10:00 AM to 9 PM depending on season; lunch and formal dinner cruises offered.
Bateaux Parisiens 01 43 26 92 55; Porte de Montebello, and 01 44 11 33 44; Pont d'Iena, provides a somewhat more luxurious cruise on their fleet of seven all-glass boats, not as big as Bateaux- Mouches. Commentary in English and French. Operates only from spring to early Fall.
Bateaux Vedettes du Pont Neuf, 01 46 33 98 58; Pont-Neuf landing stage, medium size boats, one-hour cruises
Vedettes de Paris-Ile-de France, 01 47 05 71 29; leaves from Port de Suffren, tea-dance cruises
Bat-o-Bus 01 44 11 33 44; In contrast with the cruise boats, which cater especially to thousands of tourists and provide audio commentary as well as meal service, Bat-o-Bus is more of a river transport system with five boarding points along the Seine. Operates from May to end of September.

Bus Tours

Paris-Vision 01 42 60 31 25; 214 rue de Rivoli 1st arrt. Conducts guided tours of the city and places of interest outside Paris. Brochures available at above address. Also consult Tourist Office and guidebooks listed in Appendix C for data on four other guided bus tour companies.

Car Rentals

Major U.S. rental agencies have offices in Paris which can be found either in the phone book or through the Tourist Office. Those wishing to avoid the sometimes daunting experience of driving in Paris may wish to hire a chauffeur-driven limousine. A leading agency is:

Alliance Autos 01 43 28 20 20; 94160 Sainte-Mandé 10 bis, rue Jeanne d'Arc; Bilingual drivers available.

Churches

American Cathedral in Paris 01 53 23 84 00; 23 av. George-V, 8th arrt.
Episcopalian—Numerous charity and social events
American Church 01 40 60 05 00; 65 quai d'Orsay 7th arrt.
Interdenominational Protestant (Baptist, Methodist and Presbyterian) Major gathering place for American community. The church has many activities all through the week with numerous opportunities for volunteers.

These are the two best-known American churches but seven other English language churches and synagogues can be found in the guidebooks listed in Appendix C.

Parks

Most Paris parks open their gates when the street lights go out in the morning and close when the lights go on. As noted in the text, the following list includes only some of the larger and better-known parks. Check the guidebooks in Appendix C for comprehensive data. Guided tours are given in French by the Service des Visites at 3. Av. de la Porte-d'Auteuil, 16th arrt., tel 01 40 71 75 23.

- Bois de Boulogne 01 53 92 82 82; 16th arrt. (see text for details)
- Bois de Vincennes 01 43 74 60 49; 12th arrt. This is the largest of all the parks.
- Jardin du Luxembourg 01 42 32 20 00; 6th arrt. (see text for details)
- Jardin du Palais Royal 01 47 03 92 06; 1st arrt. (see text for details)

- Jardin des Plantes 01 40 79 30 00; 5th arrt. This botanical garden was founded by Louis XIII in 1635. In 1641 Louis XIV opened the gardens to the public.
- Jardin des Tuilleries 01 40 20 90 43; 1st arrt. The quintessential French classical garden designed mainly by André Le Nôtre and recently restored to occupy a central place in the urban landscape.
- Parc André Citroen, a large park facing the Seine in the 15th arrt, built in 1993 on the site of the old Citroen plant combining classical, modern and wild landscaping
- Parc des Buttes-Chaumont 01 42 41 66 60; 19th arrt. Way off the beaten tourist track, this rather wild and romantic spot has recently undergone extensive restoration.
- Parc Monceau 01 40 71 75 23; 8th arrt. This park, a few blocks east of the Etoile, rich in fanciful landscaping and statuary as well as fake ruins.

TAXIS

Taxis are found at well-marked taxi stands throughout Paris, and it is usually easier to find a taxi there than to hail one on the street. It is helpful to check the phone number of the stand nearest your apartment and order one to come to your door. If you do so, however, be aware that the meter starts ticking from the moment of your call. (See *Paris Inside Out* for more details on taxis.)

WALKING TOURS

Our favorite guide, Sheila Hallsted, (01 30 64 97 95) is one of many English-speaking men and women who give tours. The Tourist Office provides names and contacts for others.

In addition to the pedestrian paths noted in the text it should be noted that Butterfield and Robinson now provides tapes for theme-based tours focusing on such subjects as Revolutionary Paris, Literary Cafés and Bistros, Parisian Markets, etc. Phone 800/678-1147.

Pariswalks Audio Guides provides tapes on tours of the Latin Quarter, Saint-Germain-des-Prés, and Place des Vosges. Two-cassette set $18.00. 800/748-5804

SHOPPING HOURS

Shops and Stores: The larger stores are usually closed on Sunday and Monday and open the rest of the week between 9 am and 7 pm. Many small shops, however, close between noon and 3:00 pm.

Recently store hours have become more flexible. Many food stores, for example, are staying open later. Monoprix stores stay open until 9:00 pm.

Cafés: Usual hours run from 7 am to 2 am.

Restaurants: Most close on either Sunday or Monday, more often on Sunday. After dinner closing times run from 10:30 to 1 am.

Bakers, butchers, grocery stores: Many open on Sunday, closed on Monday. In neighborhoods with several boulangeries and other food stores they usually arrange for one of each to be open every day.

Suggested Readings and Internet Web Sites

As additional help for readers interested in Parisian apartment rentals I should mention some of the numerous publications and guides that Suzanne and I have found helpful over the years. Much of the information contained in the preceding pages is based on these valuable sources. They represent only a small fraction of the large and growing number of publications on France and, in particular, Paris.

INTERNET

Voluminous amounts of information on Paris and France are now available on the Internet. A web site sponsored by the Financial Times and Volvo called Paris-Anglophone, An Anglophone's Resource on Paris, http://paris-anglo.com/home.html provides a wide range of interesting and useful data on all aspects of Parisian life. A growing number of guide books (see list below) are accessible on this web site. Renters with access to Internet should explore this as well as Parispage and Pariscope. In addition, the French Embassy web site billed as the "Gateway to French Cyberspace" is http://www.info-france-usa.org. The French Ministry of Foreign Affairs web site is http://www.france.diplomatie.fr. Basic tourist information can be obtained at http://www.francetourism.com or by phone for 50 cents a minute at 900-990-0040. Some of the publications listed below can be accessed through these web sites.

• • •

Oldest and best-known in the large field of guidebooks, of course, are the Green and Red Michelin guides published annually in French and English by Michelin Tyre Co. While we consult other guide books more and more, the two we find indispensable are the red and green Michelin. The green books covering all regions of France (one is dedicated solely to Paris) provide essential information on places of interest to visit and pertinent regional history. The red guide is famed as the donor of the coveted stars and other ratings for hotels and restaurants. We also rely heavily on the Michelin maps, which tie in with the guidebooks. There are seventeen regional maps and forty detailed maps for the entire country. These guides and maps are available in travel sections of book stores, as are the Hachette Guide to France, a Random House title, and Gault-Millau's *The Best of Paris*, which provides basic information for getting around in Paris as well as a highly regarded system of ranking hotels and restaurants. Recently Gault Millau has joined with a French travel agency to offer subscribers opportunity to dine at fine restaurants for prix fixe prices (FF 500 per person), called *Les Grandes Tables de Dégriftour Luxe*.

Several other American publishing houses put out guidebooks. We find particularly useful the Knopf Guide, *Paris*, a Borzoi imprint, $25.00, and one entitled *Paris Inside Out* offering an American expatriate's views on Parisian institutions and people, published by Houghton Mifflin, in New York $16.95 and by Parigramme in Paris. This book is one of those accessible on Paris-Anglophone web site.

Daytrips France 45 places to visit around Paris and other parts of France (includes Paris walking tours), Hastings House, UPG, Norwalk, CT, $14.95

Paris Up Close: District to District and Street by Street is a detailed and comprehensive guide to the physical layout of the city based on a unique system of isometric mapping from aerial photos. A small format packed with useful information. Passport Books, Lincolnwood, IL, $12.95

A Traveller's History of Paris by Robert Cole, Interlink Books, 1994, $13.95

A British publication, *Paupers' Paris: The Classic Guide to Getting the Most of Paris for the Fewest Francs*, by Miles Turner, (updated edition 1997) 282 pages; provides many worthwhile money-saving tips particularly useful for students and limited-budget travelers. Published by Pan Books Ltd, London SW10 9PG, about $12.00.

Zagat, the American publisher of dining guides, is planning to publish a Paris restaurant guide in 1998.

Other guidebooks that can be ordered on the Internet web site Paris-Anglophone include *Eyewitness Paris* by Dorling Kindersley, 1200 color photos, $21.95; *Paris Anglophone, 4th Edition* Complete Directory of English Speaking World in Paris, FF140; *Time Out Paris*, Everything the Visitor Needs to Make the Most of the Stay in Paris, FF110; *Food Lovers Guide to Paris*, Patricia Wells, FF110.

The Chic Shopper's Guide to Paris, Maribeth Clemente, St.Martin's Griffin, New York, $16.95

NEWSLETTERS AND PERIODICALS

FRANCE TODAY Cited above. Each issue carries interesting news and articles on France.

FRANCE A British quarterly, glossy, color illustrated, comprehensive coverage of tourism-related subjects recently offered to American readers. One year subscription $33.80.

La Belle France, The Sophisticated Guide to France, published monthly by Travel Guide, Inc. P. O. Box 3485, Charlottesville, VA, 22903-0485, FAX 804 296 0948, $87 for year's subscription. For several years we have subscribed to this newsletter which has tended in the past to concentrate on upscale hotels and restaurants catering to the tourist with deep pockets but now covers a wider range including some more moderately priced establishments. A recent issue chastised a Parisian restaurant that it had formerly praised for just being "too expensive." We find every issue has items of interest. Articles are well-researched by a knowledgeable staff whose jobs must be the envy of all their peers. Typical of the high level of their research is the article cited above, *Renting an Apartment in Paris*, which appeared in the February 1994 issue.

PARIS Notes "An Insiders Guide for Parisophiles" PO Box 3668-F, Manhattan Beach, CA 90266, Tel/FAX 310 545 2735, $39 for ten issues. An informative guide on all aspects of the city useful to all types of visitors to it.

Journal Français, a French language newspaper published monthly in a 40-page format, $35 for year's subscription. PO Box 18449, Anaheim CA 92817.

FREE PUBLICATIONS

In addition to FUSAC cited above which is free in Paris and available in the United States, there are numerous free publications obtainable in the US through the French Embassy and the Ministry of Foreign Affairs. One of the most interesting and readable is the beautifully illustrated quarterly *FRANCE* magazine containing articles on all aspect of French history, travel in areas off the beaten track and current social and cultural items of interest to Francophiles. Write *FRANCE* Magazine, Circulation Department, 4101 Reservoir Road, NW, Washington DC 20007-2182.

Each year the French Government Tourist Office also publishes *FRANCE Discovery Guide* which focuses on some aspect of French history or culture. For example, the 1997 issue dealt with travel adventures beyond the ordinary in all parts of France. Write French Government Tourist Office, 444 Madison Avenue, New York, NY 10022-6903. FAX 212 838 7855

FRANCE, Insider's News, a Quarterly Supplement to the *FRANCE Discovery Guide*, write to above address.

News from FRANCE, a semi-monthly review of news and trends in France, published by the French Embassy, address noted above.

FRANCE, a fact-filled reference book published annually by the Ministry of Foreign Affairs. 1996 edition was 264 pages. Write La Documentation Francaise, 29-31 quai Voltaire, Paris 75344

LABEL FRANCE, a quarterly color-illustrated magazine produced in English as well as French and other languages. Write Press, Information, and Communication section of Ministry of Foreign Affairs, 37 quai d'Orsay, 75007 Paris, FAX 01 43 17 52 75

$\mathscr{R}ecipes\ and\ Culinary\ Tips$

𝒯hese recipes include various dishes that Suzanne enjoys making in her own kitchen in Washington as well as simple fare appropriate for small Parisian apartment kitchens.

List of Illustrations

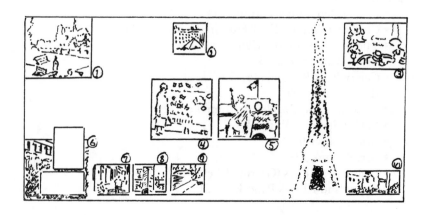

Restaurants

Le Vieux Bistro, 14 rue du Clôitre Notre-Dame, 01 43 54 18 95
Maison Fournaise, Ile des Impressionistes, Chatou, 01 30 71 41 91,
    open Wednesday through Sunday 11:00 to 5:00 PM
Fauchon, Le 30, 30 Place Madeleine, 01 47 42 56 58
Brasserie Flo, 7 cour des Ecuries, 01 47 70 13 59
La Grande Cascade, Allée de Longchamp, Bois de Boulogne,
    01 45 27 33 51
Jules Verne, second level Tour Eiffel, 01 45 55 61 44
Le Petit Laurent, 25 rue de Varenne, 01 45 48 79 64
Guirlande de Julie, 25 Place des Vosges, 01 48 87 94 07
Le Procope, 13 rue Ancienne Comédie, 01 43 26 99 20
Relais Louis XIII, rue Pont de Lodi, 01 43 26 75 96
Le Moulin de la Galette da Graziano, 83 rue Lepic, Montmartre,
    01 46 06 84 77
Café Marly, Palais du Louvre, 01 49 26 06 60
La Ferme Saint-Simon, 6 rue de Saint-Simon, 01 45 48 35 74
Potager du Roy, 1 rue du Maréchal Joffre, Versailles, 01 39 50 35 34
Brasserie du Téatre, St-Germain-en-Laye
L'Orangerie, 28 rue Saint Louis-en-l'Ile, 01 46 33 93 98
Le Beauharnais, 27 Place Napoléon, Fontainebleau, 01 64 22 32 65
Lao Tseu, 209 Boulevard St-Germain, 01 45 48 30 06

Points of Interest in Paris

Palais de Justice
Sainte-Chapelle
Conciergerie
Notre-Dame
Place Dauphine
Hôtel de Ville
The Louvre Richelieu Wing
Père Lachaise Cemetery
Bois de Boulogne and Bagatelle
Eiffel Tower
Musée des Arts Decoratifs
Church of St-Germain-des-Prés
Jardin du Luxembourg
Montmartre
Champs Elysées
Palais Royal
Shakespeare & Co.
Musée Carnavelet
Place des Vosges
Viaduc des Arts
Cluny Museum (Musée National du Moyen Age/Thermes de Cluny)
La Defense

APPENDIX H

Day Trips Outside Paris

Maison Fournaise, Chatou
Chartres
Vaux-le-Vicomte
Giverny and Musée d'Art
  Americain
Saint-Denis

Chantilly
Versailles, the Royal Vegetable
  Garden
Saint-Germain-en-Laye
Fontainebleau

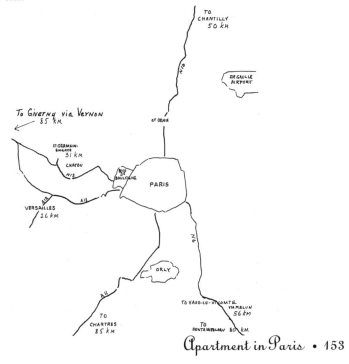

Apartment in Paris • 153

Index